AF249089

THE ART OF WILL EISNER

Written and Edited by

CATHERINE YRONWODE

With

DENIS KITCHEN

Introduction By

JULES FEIFFER

KITCHEN SINK PRESS • No. 2 SWAMP ROAD • PRINCETON • WISCONSIN • 54968

Acknowledgements

The editors would like to gratefully acknowledge
Denis McFarling and Pete Poplaski
for their assistance in the production and design of this book.
Sincere thanks are also extended to the following people for the loan
of material and help with research:

Tom Andrae, Jerry Bails, John Belfi, John Benson, David Berg, Ann Eisner, Will Eisner, Steve Englehart, Jules Feiffer, Mark Hanerfeld, Alex Kotzky, Joe Kubert, Andre Le Blanc, Darryl Lum, Denis McFarling, Klaus Nordling, Bob Palmer, Ken Pierce, Charlie Roberts, Ethan Roberts, Rodney Schroetter, Jerry Sinkovec, Calvin Slobodian, Mike Tiefenbacher, Tony Tollin, Dan Walent, Manly Wade Wellman
and
John Laney,
without whom the project would never have been possible.

Dedication

To the memory of Denny Colt (1917-1940)
"His spirit is with us still."

Library of Congress Cataloging in Publication Data

Eisner, Will
The Art of Will Eisner

1. Eisner, Will. I. Yronwode, Catherine, 1947-
II. Kitchen, Denis, 1946- . III. Title.
PN6727.E4A6 1982 741.5'092'4 [B] 82-20361
ISBN 0-87816-004-3
ISBN 0-87816-003-5 (pbk.)

Printed in United States of America.

ISBN 0-87816-003-5 paperback
ISBN 0-87816-004-3 hardcover

Contents

Introduction by Jules Feiffer

1 The Forgotten Ghetto: 1933-1936 7

2 Eisner-Iger and The Quality Shop: 1936-1941 20

3 The Spirit: 1940-1942 32

4 The War Years: 1942-1945 49

5 The Spirit and Others: 1945-1952 61

6 Commercial Art: 1951-1979 99

7 The Spirit: 1966-1981 112

8 The Remembered Ghetto: 1978-1981 129

Introduction

Will Eisner used to think he was The Spirit. Recent self-portraits indicate that he presently thinks he is Commissioner Dolan. This is maturity. I used to work for him under the name of Ebony White. "Don't draw it dis way, draw it dat way, Mist' Eisner, boss," I can recall advising him. "Shut up or I'll cut your wages," went Eisner's reply. He taught me everything I know, including not to have assistants.

Eisner, out of the limelight for years, is once again a growth industry. Ex-boy genius, innovator, entrepreneur, teacher, stingy-boss, friend, Eisner, who was written off as old-fashioned in the fifties, reemerges thirty years later as a key figure in the history of comic art and as much a personage today as he was in the days of The Spirit's appearances in the *Chicago Sun, Philadelphia Record, Parkchester Review, New York Daily Compass,* and *Washington Star,* all now gone; The Spirit outlasts them all.

Denny Colt, having laid low in Wildwood Cemetery, began to see light at the end of the culture. Out of his duplex coffin he popped to be embraced by a legion of scholarly, obsessed fans.

From *The Great Comic Book Heroes* on, Eisner has been researched, analyzed, interviewed and devoured. From "Muss 'Em Up Donovan" to *PS Magazine*, from "Hawks of the Seas" to the *American Angler,* no gravestone has been left unturned.

Through it all, Eisner remains Eisner: bemused, affable, unflappable, still out to make a buck. No one ever had to tell him how good he was and now that he is being told and told again, he is amenable but hardly impressed.

He remains ambitious and competitive, a cartoonist not out of our past but an artist who encompasses past, present and, very probably, future.

Ebony White stands comfortably at his rear. Lead on Mist' Eisner boss.

THERE, NOW... I'VE FINISHED IT!!
HEH HEH HEH

The Spirit by Feiffer; Feiffer by Eisner, from *The Spirit*, December 31, 1950 *(Deadline)*.

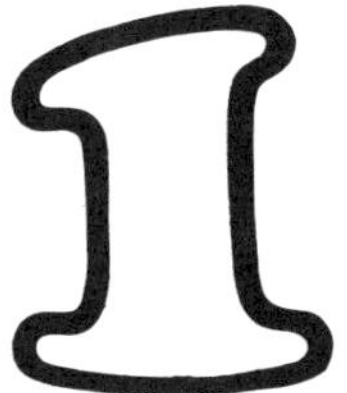

The Forgotten Ghetto: 1933-1936

Will Eisner was born on March 6, 1917, the oldest son of Jewish immigrants. His father had been a landscape painter and muralist in Austria and managed to find work painting theater backdrops for the Yiddish stage in New York. It didn't pay well though, and he drifted into the fur business, working as a cutter until the onset of the Great Depression, an event which left him and his family in grim straits — as it did the entire nation.

Young Willie, as he was then called, had to work after school and on weekends to supplement the meager family income. He sold newspapers on Wall Street. "That's when I really became interested in comics. All the great cartoonists were in the papers then — George Herriman, Alex Raymond, Milton Caniff, Elzie Segar...and it was a golden era for magazine illustration too — the pulps, of course, but also the better magazines — *Liberty, Colliers, The Saturday Evening Post.* They were full of beautiful art."

Will Eisner, circa 1926.

Although selling papers may have influenced Eisner to specialize in comics, he showed remarkable artistic talent from the age of eight. His mother, worried that he, like his father, would be unable to earn a living as a painter, tried hard to discourage him. But his father supported his interest and argued that he could always become an art teacher if he needed a regular salary. "To me art, being a syndicated cartoonist, represented a way out of the ghetto," says Will. "We were all looking for a way out. That was my primary motivation."

When the Eisner family moved from Brooklyn to The Bronx, Will entered De Witt Clinton High School. The remarkable attention this school paid to its literary and artistic curriculum is no doubt responsible for the fact that so many of its alumni have become well-known journalists, playwrights, novelists and artists. But the desire for fame, even the artistic impulse, sprang from a more basic need. "We were all looking for a way out," says Eisner. His first published drawing was printed in the high school newspaper. Its title — "The Forgotten Ghetto."

NEW YORK, FRIDAY, DECEMBER 8, 1933

AT THE "FORGOTTEN" GHETTO

Bronx's "Forgotten" Ghetto Revealed; "Is School For Crime," Doctor States

This is the third of a series of features about interesting corners of New York City.

By A. Leonard Lubunsky

A narrow street hemmed in by dark tenements....papers and bags flying round with the wind

doctor, "I think this neighborhood breeds the worst type of boys. Many boys learn all they know about crime, here."

Boys Start As Youngsters

Eisner's first published piece, *The Forgotten Ghetto*, an illustration for an article on the poverty of tenement life in The Bronx. It was printed in the De Witt Clinton high school newspaper on December 8th, 1933. Will was 15 years old at the time.

Fantasy drawing in an art deco style, 1935.

Program booklet for De Witt Clinton's "Class Nite" minstrel show, 1935. Eisner also worked on stage designs for high school plays.

Etching, 1934.

Both of these views of European towns were inspired by pictures Will found in a book owned by his father.

Pen and ink drawing, 1934.

Great White Fleet, a tempera painting for a commercial art project required in a high school art class, 1935.

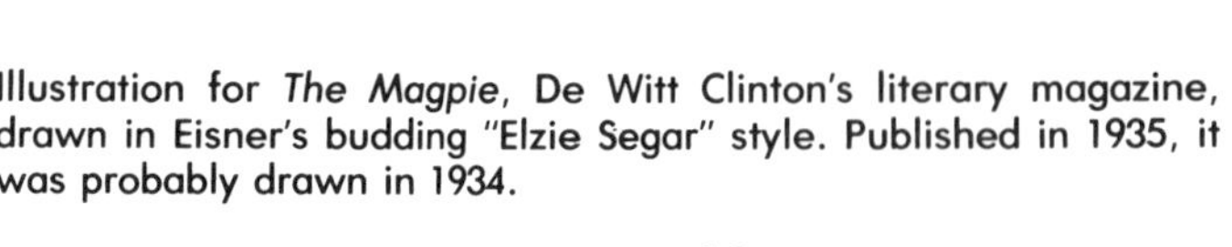

Illustration for *The Magpie*, De Witt Clinton's literary magazine, drawn in Eisner's budding "Elzie Segar" style. Published in 1935, it was probably drawn in 1934.

WHAT IS HIS NAME?

By William Eisner

A NEW STUDENT COMES TO CLINTON. SUBSCRIBE TO THE 'NEWS' AND FOLLOW HIS AMUSING ADVENTURES ALL TERM ——
IN A CORNER OF THE PUBLICATIONS OFFICE WE FIND THE ART EDITOR DRAWING THE FINAL TOUCHES ON OUR NEW FRIEND ——
HEE HEE HAW AM I FUNNY
GLUP
GOOG

AT LAST THE CARTOON IS FINISHED—AND HERE HE IS ——
HERE I COME TO GAIN SOME FAME BUT OH MY GOSH WHAT IS MY NAME?

WHAT IS HIS NAME? YOU PROBABLY HAVE A SUGGESTION. SO PLACE IT IN THE CONTEST BOX IN THE 'NEWS' OFFICE ON OR BEFORE NEXT WEDENSDAY FEB 28. THE WINNER WILL BE NAMED IN THE NEXT CARTOON AND WILL BE AWARDED 2 TICKETS TO ANY BASKETBALL GAME THIS SEASON PLUS AN ORIGINAL COLOR DRAWING OF THE CHARACTER HE NAMED.

THIS CONTEST IS OPEN ONLY TO NEWS SUBSCRIBERS!

O.K. JUST COME OVER HERE FER A MINIT
I SEE WHERE THE INDIANS BREATHE THRU ONE NOSTRIL!
OH, I SEE, A HAFF BREETH
GLUG
HEY YOU, WHATS MY NEW NAME?

YER NAME IS 'SPUNKY' SOME NAME HEY? —BY THE WAY WOULDJA DO ME A FAVOR?
SURE
PLENTY FINE NAME!

THIS IS THE IDEA— YOU GO TO THE BASKETBALL GAME TO-MORROW AND REPORT ON THE GAME TO ME SO THAT I CAN MAKE A CARTOON OF IT FOR THE NEXT ISSUE!
GEE—IM A REAL REPORTER NOW!

HAW HAW —JUS' WAIT TILL HE TRIES TO GET PAST DOC GUERNSEY!
BLESSINGS ON THEE LITTLE MAN WITH BAREFOOT CHEEKS AND EYES OF TAN!

AND NOW THE WINNER OF THE "NAME CONTEST" IS
CARMINE FIZZOLIE
SEC. 43
COME INTO THE NEWS OFFICE TO GET YOUR PRIZE, CARMINE.

CONTINUED

BEGINNER'S LUCK ? ?

BY WILLIAM EISNER

LAST WEEK SPUNKY GOT A PASS TO THE GAME FROM THE ART EDITOR; IT SEEMS THAT ITS A TRICK TO FOOL OUR PAL, SPUNKY!
HEY SPUNKY HOW ABOUT TAKIN' US WITCHA'??
SURE GINKS, C'MON ALONG!
WHEN YER TEACHER FORGETS REMEMBER THE LUNCHROOM
PUBLICATIONS

OH TEMPTATION, THOU RIDEST ME HARD! OH WELL
JUST FOLLOW ME BOYS, AND WE'LL WALK RIGHT IN, I GOT A PASS

SALAMIE! YOU AND THAT CROWD CAN'T GET IN HERE ON THAT CARD!
B-BUT DOC GUERNSEY I THOUGHT—
FLEE-HOO IM SUNK

——AND FER NO REASON AT ALL THEY JUMPED ON ME AND BEATS ME UP — S-SO KIN YOU PLEASE EXCUSE ME FROM HOMEWORK??

Weekly comic strips for *The Clintonian*, De Witt Clinton's school paper. Drawn in 1935, this was Will's first published comic strip.

I WISH I WAS A PAPER-HANGER
SNIFF

Bill Blackbeard archives

Panel from Elzie Segar's *Thimble Theatre*, January 10, 1934. The depressed figure of B. Loony Bullony, gag strip "cartoonisk" for Popeye's newspaper, the Puddleburg *Weekly Splash*, was the obvious inspiration for the self-portrait of Eisner in the second panel of the first *Spunky* strip above. Bullony was himself a self-portrait of Segar: his desire to return to the imagined carefree life of a paper-hanger harks back to Segar's childhood, when he assisted his father at that very occupation.

The End, tailpiece for *The Magpie*, 1934.

Spot illo for a school yearbook, 1934.

Spot illo for a school yearbook, 1934.

End, tailpiece for an unknown literary magazine (perhaps *The Medallion*), 1934.

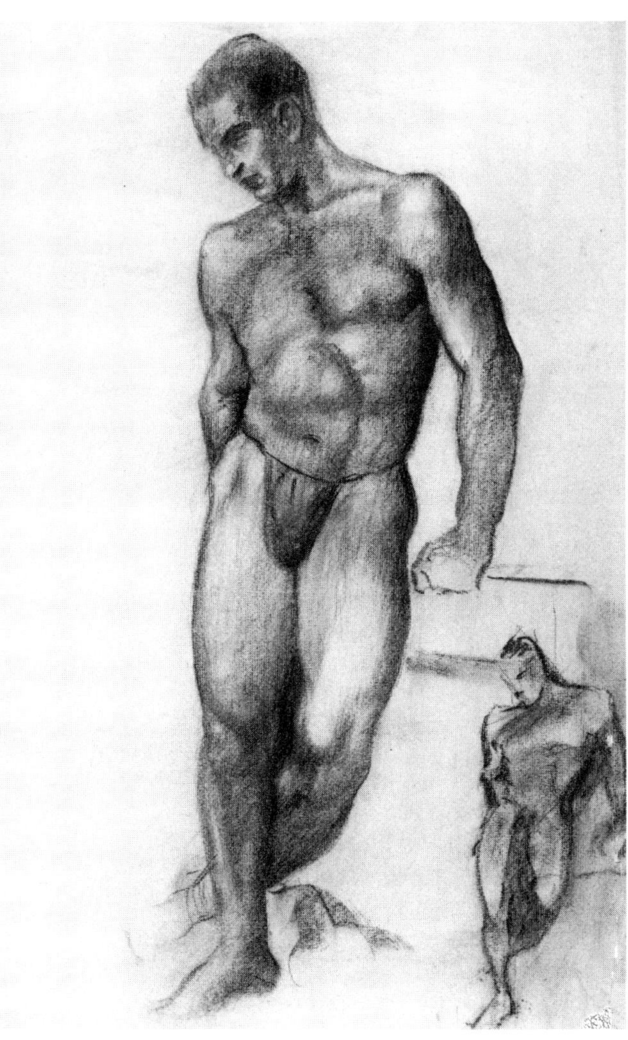

Two figure studies, charcoal, 1935.

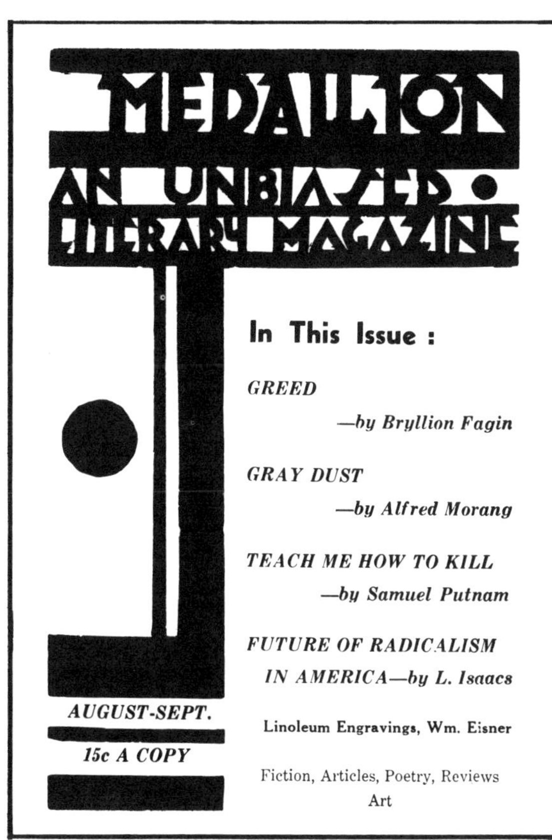

MEDALLION

AN UNBIASED LITERARY MAGAZINE

In This Issue :

GREED

—by Bryllion Fagin

GRAY DUST

—by Alfred Morang

TEACH ME HOW TO KILL

—by Samuel Putnam

FUTURE OF RADICALISM IN AMERICA—by L. Isaacs

AUGUST-SEPT.

15c A COPY

Linoleum Engravings, Wm. Eisner

Fiction, Articles, Poetry, Reviews
Art

Linoleum block cover and illustration for *The Medallion*. While still in high school, Eisner was art director of this small radical literary magazine. The issue shown (August-September, 1934) also contains a short story by *Weird Tales* author August Derleth.

-HERE I AM, 'SOUPY' McDUFF -PROMOTER -AN I CAN'T EVEN PROMOTE MESELF SOME DOUGH-I GUESS I'LL HAFTA TURN HONEST!

WATZAT

STICK EM UP-AN HAND OVER THE CASH - Y'BETTER NOT YELL

-I HOPE I CAN GET THERE IN TIME - PUFF-HERE I COME LADY-

-SAYS YOU - I DON'T LIKE HOLD-UP MEN - AND IF YOU DON'T GO AWAY-I'LL FORGET MYSELF!!
QUITE
A GENTLE OL' LADY, EH?

HEY YOU WHERE YUH GOIN WITH THAT GUN-
WHO, ME?
YAS YOU

-WHERE D'JA GIT IT-WHATCHA GONNA DO WITH IT?-GOT A LICENSE FER IT?? C'MON TALK UP
B-B-B-B

HEY--THERE YOU ARE-GIMME ME GUN - OH-COPPER-HE JUS' STOLE ME GUN -- EF I GIT ME HANDS ON YOU-
SO!!

-SO-THATS YER GUN HEY??
WHY YES
NO
Y'GOT A LICENSE FER IT??

C'MON-ALONG PEACEFUL NOW!
B-BUT LISSEN
HAW HAW- WOT LUCK

Sample strips, *Dopey and the Duke*, 1935.

By 1935, Eisner had decided that cartooning was his major artistic interest. He began to develop some sample daily strips to show the syndicates. The first of these was *Harry Carey*, a humorous detective feature.

Promo page for *Harry Carey*, 1935.

HARRY CAREY — FIRST BECAME FAMOUS AS AN UNDER COVER MAN FOR BIG INSURANCE COMPANIES.
AFTER SATISFACTORILY APPREHENDING SUCH CRIMINALS AS —
"JOE THE GYP" AND "LOONY LOOEY LUNK",
—HE WAS FORCED TO ATTEND TO VITAL PERSONAL AFFAIRS, WHICH CON- -CERNED A CERTAIN CHINESE LAUNDRYMAN NAMED 'HOLIN WAN'. THIS CRIMINAL HAD CONNIVED AND CARRIED OUT A BIG LAUNDRY SWINDLE IN WHICH HARRY UNWITTINGLY LOST HIS SHIRT. DESIRING REVENGE, AND HAVING BEEN REQUESTED BY THE AUTHORITIES TO CAPTURE THE CULPRIT, HARRY PURSUED HOLIN THRU THE DARKEST CHINATOWN, MET HIM, AND SHOT 'WAN' DEAD— — —

HARRY THEN TOOK A CORRESPONDENCE SCHOOL COURSE IN "THE ART OF BEING A SUPER SLUETH," RECEIVED A DIPLOMA, AND WENT INTO BUSINESS, AN INTERNATIONAL SUPER DETECTIVE — — HIS FIRST REALLY IMPORTANT JOB HAS COME WITH THE BOVNIAN SITUATION.

NOW WE WILL SEE HARRY CAREY IN THE GREAT BOVNIAN REVOLUTION
HO HUM -- PULL ANOTHER HAIR FROM HIS CHEST, WADSWORTH
TORTURE
—IN WHICH WE WILL SEE HARRY TORTURED MERCILESSLY BY THE CRUEL KING UMPCHAY OF BOVNIA — —
—ALSO—HARRY ESCAPING THE BOVNIAN ARMY WITH 'POSTACHIO', WHO KING UMPCHAY DROVE NUTS!!
Eisner 1935

A DE·WITT·CLINTON
- PUBLICATION -
MOSHOLU·PARKWAY·NEW YORK CITY
A. MORTIMER CLARK PRIN.
January · 1935
Eisner '34

Frontispiece for *The Magpie*, January, 1935.

Major influences on Eisner's early cartooning style included Milton Caniff, George Herriman, Alex Raymond and woodcut artist Lynd Ward — but Will freely admits that his first efforts were "a cold swipe" of Elzie Segar's *Thimble Theatre*, featuring Popeye. On these two pages and the following one of *Harry Carey* sample daily strips, both the plot and the art mimic Segar's "Spinachova" sequences.

Harry Carey promo page, 1935, establishing the locale and some of the characters in the story.

BOVNIA - OWNED BY LEM.T. FUSSBUDGET
THE GREAT APPLESAUCE CENTER OF THE WORLD AT PRESENT ON THE BRINK OF A REVOLUTION IN WHICH HARRY CAREY WILL PLAY AN IMPORTANT PART —— HERE IS A VIEW OF BOVNIA —
THIS IS BOVNIA LOTS FOR SALE CHEAP!!
THE BOVNIAN CAVALRY ALSO CHIEF SCOUT
THE ENTIRE BOVNIAN INFANTRY
TORTURE IS THE ONLY FUN I GET OUT OF LIFE
GENERAL KAIOS HEAD OF ROYAL IMPERIAL BOVNIAN ARMIES
THE KING & RULER BY DIVINE RIGHT OF ALL BOVNIA UMPCHAY THE XXXXXX
XXXXXXXXXX
Eisner '35

IN THE APARTMENT OF THE FAMOUS INTERNATIONAL DETECTIVE HARRY CAREY
—WELL I DON'T KNOW MR FUSSBUDGET — — I AM SUPPOSED TO BE ON A VACATION — —YES I KNOW BOVNIA— -A REVOLUTION ?? — THAT SOUNDS QUITE BAD —WAIT— JUST A MINUTE MR. FUSSBUDGET — —

HARRY STRIDES OVER TO THE DOOR AND FLINGS IT OPEN—
COME IN!

WELL—MR. EAVESDROPPER SPEAK UP— TALK OR I'LL
I GOT NUTTIN' TUH SAY 'XEPT DAT YOUSE'D BETTER KEEP YER NOSE OUTTA BOVNIA — IT MIGHT NOT BE 'HEALTY' FER YAH — —

—HELLO — FUSSBUDGET ?!— — —THIS IS CAREY AGAIN—WELL ABOUT THAT BOVNIAN SIT- -UATION — YOU CAN CON- -SIDER ME HIRED — —YEH I'LL COME TO YOUR HOUSE FOR FURTHER INFORMATION—
LISSEN CAREY— YER A FOOL I TELL YUH !!

AND SO HARRY CAREY EMBARKS ON ANOTHER ADVENTURE

LAST WEEK HARRY CAREY CAUGHT A MAN LISTENING AT HIS DOOR — THE MAN WARNED HARRY THAT IT WOULD BE DANGEROUS FOR HARRY TO ACCEPT THE BOVNIAN CASE OFFERED HIM BY MR. FUSSBUDGET —WHERE-UPON HARRY ACCEPTED MR. FUSSBUDGETS OFFER —
WHO IS THE EAVESDROPPER?

NOW MY FINE FRIEND, WHO ARE YOU — WHO SENT YOU HERE — AND WHY!? — YOU'D BETTER SPILL IT ALL !!
I AM A TRUSTED AND SECRET AGENT OF HIS EXALTED EXCELLENCE 'KING UMPCHAY'—OF BOVNIA DIRECT DESENDANT OF EMPEROR GLUTT THE HUNGRY'

I MIGHT TELL YOU RIGHT NOW, WE HAVE A 'SECRET POLICE,' SO COMPETENT, THAT EVERY MOVE YOU WILL MAKE, WILL INSTANTLY BE KNOWN TO OUR OFFICERS—
YEH?—WELL THAT GIVES ME AN IDEA!

WOTCHA TIE ME UP FER— WADDYUH' GONNA' DO??
—FIRST, I MUST GET SOME MORE INFORMATION, THEN, OL' SOCK, YOU ARE GOING TO BOVNIA — WITH ME!!

THE BOVNIAN SECRET AGENT HAS WARNED HARRY THAT HE WILL BE WATCHED CONSTANTLY BY HIS BOVNIAN AGENTS — THEREFORE TO BE ABLE TO GET TO MR. FUSSBUDGETS HOUSE, WITHOUT BEING SPIED UPON, HARRY HAS DE- VISED A DISGUISE.

AH—A FINE DISGUISE NO DOUBT— WHY, I COULD WALK UP TO THOSE BOVNIAN AGENTS —AND THEY WOULDN'T KNOW ME FROM ADAM

—YEP—I GOTTA HAND IT TO MESELF THIS DISGUISE IS PERFECT— —GUESS I'LL WALK IN, FUSSBUDGET WON'T KNOW ME WITH THIS PHONEY BEARD ON— HA-HA —I'LL BET IT'LL SCARE HIM PLENTY—THE BUTLER SURELY WON'T KNOW ME, IT'LL BE A CINCH— HEH-HEH—

MR. FUSSBUDGET'S EXPECTING YOU MR. CAREY— 'OW I SAY, WHY THE CHIN WHISKERS MR. CAREY, 'AV YOU A COLD?
?!

GOOD DISGUISE PAH!!
NOW I WONDER 'AVE I OFFENDED 'IM ??— —I STILL CAWN'T SEE WHY 'E WORE A BEARD !?

Above, three sample dailies, *Harry Carey*, 1935. This appears to have been Eisner's first attempt at doing the story. It was too wordy and the pacing was too fast for a daily strip.

Below, the first day of Eisner's second attempt at a *Harry Carey* series, 1935. The pacing is much slower and the action takes up some of the burden originally given to the words. (Continued on the next page.)

OUR SCENE OPENS IN THE HOTEL SUITE OF THE WEALTHY AND INTERNATIONALLY FAMOUS — LEMUEL TIFFET FUSSBUDGET —
A MR. HARRY CAREY TO SEE YOU SIR
SEND HIM IN HERMAN—
YES SIR — I'M PLEASED TO MEET YOU
SO YOU ARE THE FAMOUS HARRY CAREY
—MY BOY, I HAVE CHOSEN YOU FROM AMONGST MANY OUTSTANDING DETECTIVES — HOWEVER YOUR EXPERIENCE SUITS MY PURPOSE BEST— —ARE YOU FAMILIAR WITH A SMALL COUNTRY NAMED BOVNIA—??
WELL NO—BUT I HAVE HEARD OF IT—A HAVEN FOR CRIMINALS
FUSSBUDGT'S STORY IN THE NEXT INSTALLMENT

BOVNIA IS THE GREATEST APPLESAUCE MAKING COUNTRY IN THE WORLD — IN THE PAST, I HAVE BUILT AND FINANCED ENORMOUS APPLE--SAUCE FACTORIES THRU WHICH BOVNIA HAS PROSPERED —AHEM ALSO MYSELF—RECENTLY HOWEVER, THE KING OF BOVNIA AND HIS PRIME-MINISTER HAVE TAKEN OVER AB--SOLUTE CONTROL, IMPORTED MANY EX-CONVICTS—AND HAVE SET ABOUT FULFILLING A HORRIBLE SCHEME.

—THEY INTEND TO BEGIN INVADING SEVERAL OF THE SMALLER AND INDEPENDENT REALMS WHICH SURROUND THEM. THEY HAVE AL--READY CAPTURED MY FACTORIES AND THEY'RE USING THE REVENUE TO ——
STOP! SHHH!!! I THINK WE HAVE A VISITOR

COME IN!

WHO IS THE EAVES-DROPPER

WE'VE GOT YUH, NOW TALK!
HARRY SEIZES THE STRANGER — AND QUESTIONES HIM — — —

—I GOT NUTIN' TU SAY 'XEPT DAT YOUS'D BETTER KEEP YER NOSE OUTA BOVNIA!
WHO ARE YOU—AND WHAT'S THE BIG IDEA!!
?

IT APPEARS—LOOK HARRY!—GOING OUT THE WINDOW ——HE'LL ESCAPE
HEY!! WOTN YOU STOP!! HEY!!

WE CANT CATCH HIM NOW, —BOY HE'S FAST,— Y'KNOW MR. FUSSBUDGET,—I'M INTERESTED — CONSIDER ME HIRED!
HOT DAWG
BAN

And so HARRY CAREY EMBARKS — ON A NEW ADVENTURE

Above, the second and third days of the second series of *Harry Carey* sample dailies, 1935.

Below, sample daily strips, *The Flame*, 1935.

BIGGEST GEM TH IN YEARS, SAY POLICE, 'FINGERS' MORAN FREED
LACK OF EVIDENCE RELEASED, TO-DAY, THE NOTORIOUS UNDERWORLD CHARACTER, 'FINGERS' MORAN. MORAN WAS SUSPECTED BY THE POLICE,
HE HOWEVER PRODUCED EXCELLENT EVIDENCE OF HIS WHERE ABOUTS THE NIGHT OF EM ROBBERY
COLT GEMS STOLEN

AMID THE CLATTER AND EXCITEMENT OF THE CITY STREETS — —WE FOLLOW THREE MEN TO THE FAMOUS CARLTON HOTEL — THRU THE LOBBY AND THEN TO THE ELEVATOR —

—OH IT'S YOU—C'MON IN BOYS
—UP—TO THE PENTHOUSE — WHERE THEY KNOCK — — THE DOOR IS SLOWLY OPEND —

'FINGERS' MORAN
—AS USUAL, HE HAS A PERFECT ALIBI — WITNESSES ARE ALWAYS ON HAND TO TESTIFY FOR HIM —

—YEH—A BOTTLE OF YER BEST CORN AND GRUB—PRONTO!

— GENTLEMEN — THESE ARE THE COLT JEWELS —YES THE STUFF THAT'S JUST BEEN STOLEN— THEY ARE DANGEROUS — TO ME, BUT TO YOU, WHO ARE IN A POSITION TO DISPOSE OF THEM QUICKLY, THEY ARE EXTREMELY VALUABLE —FOR SALE TO THE HIGHEST BIDDER—

COME IN!
—SUDDENLY—A KNOCK ON THE DOOR— IN -STANTLY THE GEMS ARE HIDDEN — THE MEN SILENTLY CONCEAL THEMSELVES— —AND WAIT FOR THE VISITOR—

A WAITER ENTERS!

—IT'S O.K. BOYS C'MON OUT— —ONLY THE WAITER WID THE CHOW

—YES GENTS— ONLY THE WAITER— —NOW PUT UP YOUR HANDS!! —AND I WARN YOU MY TRIGGER FINGER IS VERY SENSATIVE — MORAN, GET ME THOSE JEWELS!—

BANG
—A GUN IS DRAWN— — THE STRANGER FIRES!!

—YOU LEARN ONLY BY EXPERIENCE —TCH-TCH OH WELL — I HATE TO TAKE THESE ROCKS FROM YOU — BUT I HAPPEN TO NEED A NEW PAIR OF SHOES JUST NOW — MUCH OBLIGED GENTS —— GOOD NIGHT MORAN!—

—OH YES, WHEN THE REAL WAITER COMES TO—GIVE HIM AN ICE BAG I HIT HIM HARD

A THIEF WHO DARES TO STEAL LOOT EVEN FROM 'FINGERS' MORAN
A DANGEROUS GAME

Tetley Tea advertisement, *Eve* magazine, Vol. 1, No. 1 (April, 1934).

Story illustration, *Eve* magazine, Vol. 1, No. 1 (April, 1934). This artwork was credited to "Julian Willi," a pseudonym composed of Eisner's own first name and that of his younger brother (who was, ironically, known to his family and friends as Pete).

Spot illos, *Eve* magazine, Vol. 1, No. 1 (April, 1934).

BOY OH BOY, ARE MY HANDS ALL GRIMY! AND I'M GOING OUT TO-NIGHT TOO!
THA'S O.K. JUS' GET A CAN OF GRE-SOLVENT AND IT'LL CLEAN YUH UP IN A JIFFY -
SAY SPIKE, I'LL GET YUH A CAN OF GRE-SOLVENT, Y'LL NEED IT!!
OH DARN!! I'VE GOT MY HANDS DIRTY FROM THIS TYPEWRITER!
AW GET YERSELF A CAN OF GRE-SOLVENT MY GOIL USES NUTHIN ELSE -
I USE GRE-SOLVENT FOR CLEAN HANDS, BUT HOW I LOVE IT FOR KITCHEN-UTENSILS AND THE BATHROOM TOO!
YOU SPOILED MY BEST GUEST TOWEL, FROM NOW ON YOU USE GRE-SOLVENT
YES DEAR TO BE SURE
PARDON ME MY GOOD LADY, BUT I'VE BEEN RIDIN' DE RAILS ALL NIGHT, COULD YUH STAKE ME TO A CAN UV GRE-SOLVENT TO CLEANUP WID?
YEP, BY HECK, I SHORE DON'T MIND A MITE BEIN' DIRTIED UP, GOOD OL' GRE-SOLVENT WILL CLEAN ME UP SWELL!
HEY POP, Y'FERGOT YR GRE-SOLVENT

Sketched from Life, Gre-Solvent brochure, 1934.

While developing his cartooning style, Eisner took a job in a print shop, where he worked as a printer's assistant. He then got a job in the ad department of the *New York American*, writing copy, supplying spot illos and doing layouts. His first paid artwork was for a small Gre-Solvent booklet at left. Entitled *Sketched From Life*, it gave eight examples of the product's usefulness. This brochure was designed for inclusion in packages of the cleanser, whose motto was, "where there's life, there's soap."

Eisner's big break, or so he thought, came when he was hired as art director for the fledgling *Eve* magazine ("Dedicated to the modern American Jewess"). The periodical was beset with difficulties from the first, not the least of which was the youthful Eisner's propensity for scattering pictures of prizefighters and gun molls among the articles on dainty salads and new spring fashions. He was fired, but had the satisfaction of seeing *Eve* fold a few months later.

A photo, taken in 1941, of Eisner standing in front of an untitled oil painting completed in 1936. His studies at the Art Students League under George Bridgman, the great anatomist, and painter Robert Brachman had a beneficial effect on his life drawing skills and supplied the basic anatomical and architectural realism underlying his mature cartooning style.

2 Eisner-Iger and The Quality Shop: 1936-1941

Eisner broke into the fledgling comic book field in 1936. His first comics appeared in John Henle's *Wow, What A Magazine!*, a title which lasted only four issues before folding. *Harry Carey*, the feature Will had created while still in high school, made its brief professional bow here, under the title *Harry Karry*. The new name was probably chosen to avoid confusion with cowboy actor Harry Carey, since the plot centered on a slapstick detective, not a western hero.

The Flame, Eisner's high school detective strip, also made a debut of sorts in *Wow* — but it had become a buccaneer series somehow, with only the name — and the hero's blond good looks — unchanged. Unlike *Harry Karry*, which followed the plotline originally conceived by Eisner in 1935, the revised *Flame* strip was an ambitious project involving a large cast of characters and a well-researched historical locale. When it was terminated after only four episodes, Eisner did the obvious thing: he found another publisher and started all over again with the same story line, the same blond hero — and a new name, *Hawks of the Seas*.

Henle published work by Will's school friend, Bob Kane, and also featured the cartoons of Samuel "Jerry" Iger. When *Wow* collapsed, Eisner and Iger formed a partnership, hiring Kane and a few other artists to work in their shop. Among those who joined them were Lou Fine and Jack Kurtzberg, the latter better known today as Jack Kirby. The Eisner-Iger studio was run like a factory. The going page rate for finished script and art was five dollars, and nobody but the incorrigibly perfectionistic Lou Fine was willing to spend overtime on fancy feathering techniques.

The company created a syndicate, Universal Phoenix Features, to market their output overseas. American newspaper strips were being reprinted abroad at a tremendous rate. By making their new work look like Sunday comic pages, Eisner and Iger managed to sell it to foreign markets before it ever appeared at home. And, if the truth be known, much of it was too crude to ever have competed against such sophisticated American strips as *Terry and the Pirates* and *Prince Valiant*.

The earliest Eisner-Iger shop strips appeared in the British and Australian editions of *Wags*, a weekly tabloid reprint paper. However, within a year, the material was being sold to American comic book publishers like T. T. Scott of Fiction House and Victor Fox of Fox Comics. Because the page layouts for the comic books were different than the fake "Sunday page" format originally used, a great deal of the artwork was actually cut apart panel by panel and pasted up in altered form. Dialogue was rewritten if necessary and often extra bridging panels were added to fill out the pages. Thus few Americans have ever seen Eisner's early work in its original form — and because *Wags* is one of the rarest comics around, even foreign fans have no access to the material.

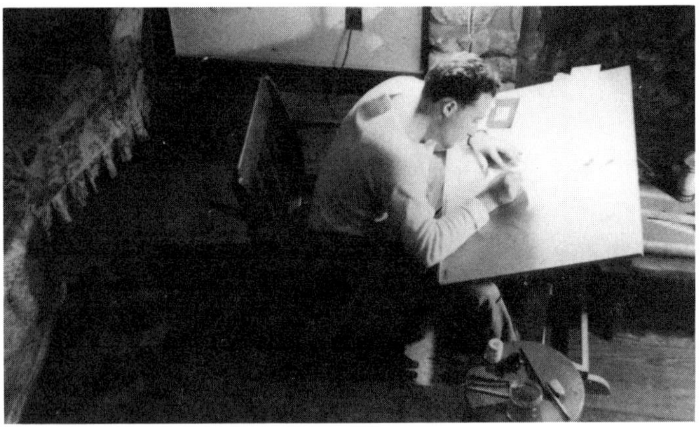

Eisner at a summer cabin on Lake Mohansic, N.Y., drawing Hawks of the Seas, 1937.

Eisner produced an enormous quantity of work during this period, drawing in half a dozen styles under two dozen aliases. He also scripted and layed out stories for other artists in the studio to draw, particularly Lou Fine, whose style was fairly close to his at this point in time. As editor/art director for the shop, Will was never shy about imposing his approach onto the submitted pages. Stories by Jack Kirby, Lou Fine, Bob Kane, Mort Meskin and others display the occasional Eisner panel, presumably pasted over the original work. Will was influenced by Milton Caniff in regard to the use of "camera angles," and as his facility increased, he became more and more baroque in his use of through-the-window and up-from-the-floor shots. His effect on those who worked with him gave Eisner-Iger material a distinct shop "look" which lasted well beyond his association with the company.

In 1939 Eisner was approached by Everett M. "Busy" Arnold of Quality Comics Group to produce a 16 page newspaper supplement for the Des Moines Register-Tribune Syndicate. Eisner agreed and dissolved his partnership with Iger at once. He joined Quality Comics as a scripter, artist, idea man and editor. In addition to this, he originated *The Spirit, Lady Luck* and *Mr. Mystic* for the newspaper supplement. While at Quality he was responsible for the creation of a host of the company's most popular features, among them *Dollman, The Black Condor, Uncle Sam, Espionage* and *Blackhawk*. Typically he would script and draw the first issue or two, then fall back to scripting and laying out the work for another artist to finish. Ultimately he would hand the entire feature over to a scripter like Audrey "Toni" Blum or Dick French and an artist chosen from the Quality staff, such as Lou Fine, Paul Gustafson, Bob Powell, Nicholas Viscardi, Reed Crandall, Chuck Mazoujian, Fred Guardineer or Chuck Cuidera, merely editing the finished product to his own standards, and thus preserving its "Eisnerian" look.

A COMPLETE STORY
'TOP-HAND'
A 'WILD TEX' MARTIN STORY
BY
WILLIAM EISNER
THE PEACEFUL SILENCE OF 'DUSTY FORKS' IS SUDDENLY SHATTERED AS A HORSEMAN RIDES WILDLY INTO TOWN —

Wild Tex Martin splash panel from *Keen Detective Funnies* Vol. 1 No. 9 (Centaur, August, 1938).

BATTLING NELSON
NELSON'S PULSE NEVER WENT ABOVE 40 EVEN DURING A FIGHT!
THE NORMAL PULSE BEAT FOR ADULTS IS 70.
FISTIC FAX
A WET GLOVE CAN CUT A FIGHTER'S FACE LIKE A KNIFE
I DON'T WANNA FIGHT, I WANNA SHAKE HANDS
WILLIE HOPPE
EX-BILLIARD CHAMP SHAKES HANDS WITH HIS CLENCHED FIST—TO PREVENT A WRENCHED CUE-FINGER —
Erwin
LEONORE KNIGHT
SWIMMING CHAMP—BELIEVES THAT SHARKS IN THE WATER IS GOOD LUCK!

Sports Shorts, signed "Erwin," from *Jumbo Comics* (Fiction House, 1939).

Watercolour character studies for proposed comic features, circa 1937. It is possible these were intended as samples for Centaur, as the company published titles in the three genres shown (detective, western and sports).

COMICS ★ STORIES ★ STAMPS ★ 'PLANES
WOW
WHAT A MAGAZINE!
SEPT
10¢
IN THIS ISSUE
JACK DEMPSEY WRITES ABOUT POPEYE'S PUNCH
BOB RIPLEY BELIEVE IT OR NOT
MORE ADVENTURES OF FU MANCHU
LITTLE KING OTTO SOGLOW
CHAPTER 3 SCOTT DALTON
AND OTHER Thrilling Cartoons

Cover, *Wow What A Magazine!* No. 3 (David McKay, September, 1936), featuring *Harry Karry*.

JUMBO COMICS
No. 4 DEC.
10¢ Bigger & Better Funnies 10¢
JUMBO COMICS FEATURES:
HAPPY DAYS
JUMBO JIM'S PRIZE PARTY
HOT DAWG! DRUMSTICKS AN' GRAVY!
GANGWAY! I'M LEAVIN' TOWN FOR THE HOLIDAYS!
HAWKS OF THE SEAS
WATER, WATER, I THIRST!
AW SHUX!
HUNCHBACK OF NOTRE DAME
ALSO SHEENA, WILTON OF THE WEST, SPENCER STEEL, PUZZLES, JEST LAFFS, DR. HAYWARD, MODERN PLANES AND MANY OTHER FAVORITES....
BIG PAGES—BIG PICTURES—BIG TYPE—EASY TO READ

Cover, *Jumbo Comics* No. 4 (Fiction House, December, 1938).

JUMBO COMICS
No. 6 FEB.
10¢ Bigger & Better Funnies 10¢
JUMBO COMICS FEATURES:
WILTON OF THE WEST
HAWKS OF THE SEAS
BOY! WAS THAT COP SORE! IT'S A GOOD THING HE DOESN'T KNOW WHERE WE'RE HIDING!
WHOOPS! THERE'S DEAH LITTLE CHAUNCEY SYLVESTER--- HERE'S ONE FOR HIS KISSER!
SHEENA · DR. HAYWARD · ZX-5
BIG PAGES—BIG PICTURES—BIG TYPE—EASY TO READ

Cover, *Jumbo Comics* No. 6 (Fiction House, February, 1939).

Fill-In-The-Balloon Contest, *Jumbo Comics* No. 6 (Fiction House, February, 1939).

YARKO
THE
GREAT

OUR SCENE OPENS IN THE BUSY NEW YORK HARBOR, CROSSROADS OF THE WORLD.... MID CLOUDS OF SMOKE FROM A MYRIAD OF CHUGGING TUGS THE SUPER LINER TANORA GLIDES HOME...

YOUR LUGGAGE HAS BEEN CHECKED FOR SMUGGLED ARTICLES--- YOU MAY LEAVE NOW, MRS. LAWTON
THANK YOU, INSPECTOR
SECTIO
2A

MRS LAWTON HEADS FOR A WAITING LIMOUSINE..
HOME, JAMES--

ROCO! WHAT ARE YOU DOING HERE?
I CAME TO GREET YOU---

---AND BY THE WAY, HAND OVER THE ROCK YOU SMUGGLED IN----
THE WOMAN STOOPS OVER AND REMOVES HER SHOE........

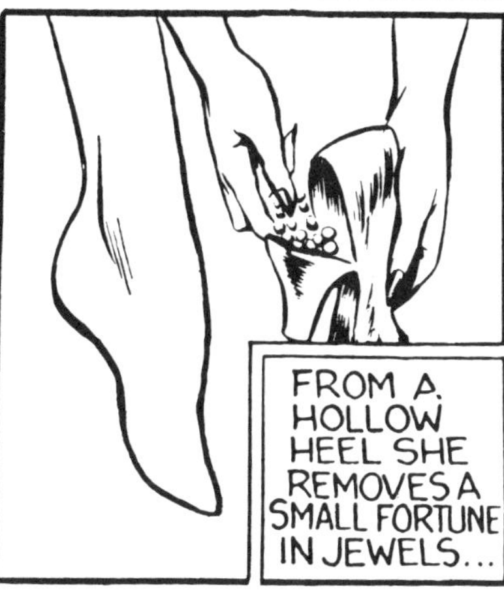
FROM A HOLLOW HEEL SHE REMOVES A SMALL FORTUNE IN JEWELS...

ROCCO, THIS IS THE LAST TIME-- I'M AFRAID MY HUSBAND SUSPECTS I'VE BEEN SMUGGLING JEWELRY
DON'T WORRY, I'LL TAKE CARE OF EVERY-THING!

IN THE LAWTON HOME, YARKO IS CHATTING WITH HIS OLD FRIEND, JUDGE LAWTON......
--AND I BROUGHT HIM DOWN WITH ONE SHOT---
PAWDON, SIR--YOUR WIFE HAS JUST ARRIVED---

HELLO, FRED DARLING
HELLO, MY DEAR-- THIS IS MY OLD FRIEND, YARKO
DELIGHTED, MADAM---
18

Yarko the Great, Master Magician. This series first saw print in the Australian comic, *Wags*, but was later reprinted in Fox's *Wonderworld*, in cut-up form. *Yarko* was the direct predecessor of *Mr. Mystic*, a Bob Powell-illustrated feature Eisner created for *The Spirit Section* in 1940.

One of the most talked-about but least-seen of Eisner's early comic book features has been the one-shot *Muss 'Em Up*, which appeared in Centaur's *Funny Pages* in 1938 and was reprinted in *Keen Detective Funnies* and *Little Giant Detective Funnies* in 1939. Because Jules Feiffer devoted quite a lot of space to a description of the story in his 1965 book, *The Great Comic Book Heroes,* there has been continuous fan interest in it. Said Feiffer of this early and admittedly crude work:

"*Muss 'Em Up* was full of dark shadows, creepy angle shots, graphic close-ups of violence and terror... Eisner's line had weight. When one Eisner character slugged another, a real fist hit real flesh. Violence was no externalized plot exercise, it was the gut of his style. Massive and indigestible, it curdled, lava-like, from the page."

A COMPLETE STORY
MUSS 'EM UP
BY WILLIAM EISNER
TONY, HERE, IS DEAD --I'M BOSS NOW!-- ANY BODY DONT LIKE IT ??--
-S-SURE YER TOPS WID US----BOSS!
-THE HEADQUARTERS OF A SMALL GANG-

OCT. 1ST.
GOT ALL DE DOUGH BOYS ???
YEH! C'MON BOSS DE OL' MAN'S TOO SCAIRT TO DO ANY THING- -- WE'LL JUS' TIE HIM UP!!
-WELL- I'LL JUST MAKE SURE--YOU'RE TOO OLD TO LIVE MISTER!! -AN' I DON'T LIKE YOUR FACE!!!
BANG!
OCT.10
BANK
TAKE YER TIME IN THERE BOYS - DIS COP WONT BOTHER US
OCT.20
SO- YOU RECOGNIZE ME EH?? WAL AINT DAT NICE!!--
DEC.8
-I TOLD YOU NOT TO MAKE ANY NOISE!!---I'LL BE RIGHT 'WITCHA' BOYS--
BANG
P1

KILLER AT LARGE!
POLICE ARE BAFFLED!
IDENTITY OF KILLER STILL UNKNOWN
HEY BOYS!! --- -DIDJA' SEE DIS -- --I'M STILL AT LARGE -HAW-HAW-HAW-- -WELL I SHOULD BE-- --EVERYBODY WOTS SEEN ME IS DEAD!! HAW HAW HAW!!!

-YEA- DATS JUST DA TROUBLE--WE' BEEN BUMPIN PEOPLE LIKE FLIES--'AN MOST OF 'EM COPS TOO!!
'SMATTER GITTIN' YALLER CURLEY?!

NAW--YOU KNOW ME BETTERN DAT!-- BUT- I'M NO KILLER!-AN I AINT GONNA BOIN' JUS' BECAUSE YOU GOT AN ITCHY TRIGGER FINGER!!
SO WHAT?!

SO--I'M QUITTIN'! I'LL BE SEEIN YUH-- --IN DE HOT SEAT--

SO-LONG CURLY!!
P2

DERE'S ONLY ONLY ONE WAY TO QUIT DIS GANG --DAT'S DE WAY----ANY BODY WANNA QUIT? ----NO?---O.K THEN- GET RID OF THE STIFF!
BANG!

YES SIR ??
SEND CAPTAIN SPENCER IN TO ME---AND I'LL BE IN CON-FERENCE ALL AFTERNOON
EDITORIAL
ITS ABOUT TIME THE POLICE DID SOME THING ABOUT THESE RECENT KILLINGS OUR POLICE FORCE HAVE DONE NOTHING TO APPREHEND THIS FIEND

--DID YOU READ THIS SPENCER ?!-WHY-THIS- -I-ITS DEPLORABLE-WHAT'S HAPPENED TO THE FORCE ASLEEP???
I'VE READ IT SIR

AY- AND IT'S THE TRUTH THEY PRINT-- WE HAVEN'T GOT A CLUE SIR!!-- SURE-THE UNDERWORLD CAN TELL US- BUT THEY WONT!- THEY'RE SCARED OF HIM--THERE IS ONLY ONE WAY TO GET THE INFORMATION WE WANT--BUT WE'RE HAMPERED BY A LOT OF PETTY LAWS!!!

-IN MY OPINION THERE IS ONLY ONE MAN IN THIS TOWN THAT CAN GET US WHAT WE WANT-- HE'S "HAMMER DONOVAN"
WELL ??- WELL WHY HAVEN'T YOU ASSIGNED HIM TO THIS CASE -THIS IS A VERY IMPORTANT--

-YOU THREW HIM OFF THE FORCE FOR BEATING UP "WILLIE THE MOUSE"- BUT I THINK HE'LL COME BACK AND TAKE THE ASSIGNMENT--IF--YOU ASK HIM- AND GIVE HIM A FREE HAND"

-HMM- YES I REMEMBER NOW- I DIDN'T WANT TO REMOVE HIM- IT WAS "WILLIES" LAWYER--HE HAD POLITICAL IN-FLUENCE----BUT I'LL EVEN RISK MY JOB AND RETURN HIM TO THE FORCE-- IF HE CAN CRACK THIS CASE-- -AND- MY ORDERS NOW ARE-- MUSS 'EM UP!! I GIVE DONOVAN FULL AUTHORITY!
P3

WELL, WELL, WELL MY BOY HOW DOES IT FEEL TO BE BACK AND WORKING WITH US AGAIN ??
SWELL-AND YOU KNOW IT

---AND THAT'S THE STORY--THESE KILLINGS MUST BE STOPPED---AND WE HAVEN'T A SINGLE CLUE!!

-NOW-THAT'S WHY WE'VE GOT YOU-THE UNDER-WORLD KNOWS WHO AND WHERE THIS KILLER IS--- YOU HAVE A 'FREE HAND' DO ANYTHING YOU WANT-BUT GET THAT KILLER!

NOW-WHAT'S YOUR FIRST MOVE
-RAID EVERY 'JOINT' IN TOWN--DRAG IN ALL THE KNOWN CROOKS--- WE'LL 'HAMMER' THE INFORMATION OUT OF THEM!!

C'MON TALK YOU CROOK OR I'LL--
-I-I-WONT-- DO WOTCHA LIKE TO ME-IT AINT NUTHIN' TO WOT'LL HAPPEN TO ME IF I SQUEAL!!
P.4

ALL-RIGHT--ALL-RIGHT- I'LL LET YOU GO--BUT YOU CAN TELL THE REST OF THE UNDER--WORLD RATS THIS--- I'M COMING AFTER THIS KILLER MYSELF--AND WHEN I GET MY HANDS ON HIM---

-HAMMER DONOVAN'S HOME THE NEXT MORNING --
-HELLO--YES HEADQUARTERS THIS IS DONOVAN-WHAT?? ANOTHER MURDER?--DID YOU QUESTION THE DYING WITNESS?--SO-----IT'S MIKE MOARELLI EH? ---WELL NOW WE'VE AT LEAST GOT SOMETHING TO WORK ON!! ---
YES--I'M GOING OUT TO GET HIM!! -BLOCK ALL HIGHWAY'S IN-AND-OUT OF THE CITY--COVER THE SHIPPING AND RAIL DEPOTS-- THATS ALL UNTIL YOU NEXT HEAR FROM ME-- ---THANKS
GOING OUT BY SELF?
YES FEN SOO--GOING RAT HUNTING--IT'S MIKE MOAR-ELLI--I'M ITCHING TO TAKE A CRACK AT HIM?-WELL HERE GOES NOTHING-!!
THUS MORNING PASSES WEARILY INTO EVENING-AS HAMMER CONTINUES HIS SEARCH--
C'MON SPILL!!-WHERE IS MIKE??
'CHEEZ'-DON'T HIT ME NO MORE DONOVAN! -HONES' I'M TELLIN'YUH DE' TRUTH-I DONT KNOW WHERE HE IS-- I SWEAR IT!!
HONEST BOSS I AINT SEEN HIM NO PLACE
IT HAD BETTER BE THE TRUTH!!
WELL--WELL--WELL IF IT ISNT 'HOPHEAD HARRY'--HOWS THE DOPE BUSINESS?
WOTCHA WANT WID ME--I AINT DONE NUTHIN!!
-I'M LOOKING FOR MIKE MOARELLI-YOU KNOW WHERE HE IS-AND YOUR GOING TO TELL ME BECAUSE IF YOU DONT--WELL-I HEAR THAT THE NARCOTIC SQUAD IS LOOKING FOR YOU-WELL--DO I GET THE INFO??
-P-PLEASE DONT--I'LL TALK--HHES HIDIN' OUT IN BACK O'MOONY'S GARAGE-D--DONT TELL 'EM WILLYUH DEY'LL KILL ME SSSURE!
P.5

THANKS HARRY--YOU KNOW THAT I WONT SELL YOU OUT--- THIS IS PROBABLY THE FIRST DECENT THING YOU'VE EVER DONE----

HMM-'MOONY'S GARAGE--A LIKELY HIDEOUT--NOW FOR A PHONE BOOTH AND THEN--
MOONY'S
-A SHORT TIME LATER

HELLO--HEADQUARTERS-- DONOVAN SPEAKING--YES-I HAVE FOUND MOARELLI'S HIDEOUT--I'M GOING UP TO GET HIM-NOW!--IS THAT WITNESS STILL ALIVE-GOOD I'LL CALL YOU AGAIN--WHEN I HAVE MIKE!!

WELL-WELL-COME RIGHT IN ----COPPER!!
P6

-A SLY SMILE APPEARS ON MIKE'S FACE AS HE SEES THAT HAMMER DONOVAN IS ALONE ---

GOOD EVENING MIKE I JUST--

-SUDDENLY 'HAMMER' SPINS AROUND AND FIRES AT A FIGURE CONCEALED BEHIND A DRAPERY ---

DROP THAT GAT AND SAY YOUR PRAYERS!!
THAT'S ALL I WANT TO KNOW!!---

GET UP AND FIGHT--YOU YELLOW LIVERED MURDERER!!
-O.K.-C-C-COPPER-YOU W-WIN--

HELLO-HELLO-HEADQUARTERS-DONOVAN AGAIN--I'VE GOT MOARELLI--YES I'M ALL RIGHT THANKS---GET THE 'HOT SEAT WARMED UP!--AND-OH YES---
SEND AN AMBULANCE FOR MIKE AND HIS PAL--THEY WERE RESISTING AN OFFICER--SO I SORT OF MUSSED 'EM UP!!
P7
THE END

HAWKS OF THE SEAS
BY Willis Rensie
MERRYSTONE'S SOLDIERS ARE PLANNING TO ATTACK THE HAWK'S SHIP AT DAWN ---
DARKNESS ENVELOPES INAGUA WITH TROPICAL SUDDENESS, AND AS THE TOWN'S TWINKLING LIGHTS SLOWLY DISAPPEAR AN UNNATURAL SILENCE FILLS THE HARBOUR ----
ANCHORED TO A PIER LAPPING THE SILENT WATERS, A SLAVE SHIP LIES AT REST WAITING TO LAND HER HUMAN CARGO.
YOUR TURN ON WATCH MONK!.. I'M GLAD YOU'VE GOT THIS TRICK --- THOSE BLACKS SINGING..UGH!!
..PFAW! THEY DON'T BOTHER ME, I'VE A WAY TO SILENCE 'EM.
NOT THE ---?
YES! --- WATCH ME, I'LL SHOW YE!
CRACK
STOP YOUR INFERNAL SINGIN'! --- IT'S MONK WOT'S ON DUTY NOW..SO YE'D BETTER SHUT UP.
HUH! --- THAT'LL LARN 'EM ---- THEY KNOW WHO'S BOSS HERE. HA! HA! HA!
...YOU!! W..WHAT ARE YOU DOING HERE ??---
HELP! --- ALL HANDS ON DECK! IT'S --- IT'S! ----
43

Hawks of the Seas, page 43. This feature, in which Eisner first began to develop his sophisticated approach to page layout and panel breakdown, was originally conceived as 123 numbered "Sunday" pages. It was first published in the Australian and British editions of *Wags* in 1937, but was soon reprinted in Fiction House's *Jumbo Comics*.

HAWKS OF THE SEAS
BY Willis Rensie
THE HAWK HAS CLIMBED THE REAR WALL OF THE TINY GARRISON THEY ARE PREPARING TO STORM
I WASN'T SEEN.....NOW TO GET THE REST OF THE MEN UP......
EAGER HANDS REACH OUT OF THE ROLLING WAVES TO GRASP THE DESCENDING ROPE.
A MOMENT LATER 10 MEN HOIST THEMSELVES OUT OF THE ROLLING SEA.......
ABOUT TURN!! THEY'VE COME UP BEHIND US... ..... ABOUT TURN!!
INSTANTLY THE MEN CLOSE IN BATTLE....
AND, AS THE TIDE OF BATTLE SLOWLY TURNS
WHERE'S MERRYSTONE? I MUST GET HIM BEFORE MY MEN TEAR HIM TO PIECES!
THE COWARD! .....HE'S ABSCONDED.
49

Hawks of the Seas, Page 49. The plot of *Hawks* was, according to Eisner, "my idea of a Douglas Fairbanks or Erroll Flynn movie on paper." There's a healthy serving of Robert Louis Stevenson's *Treasure Island* thrown in for good measure as well.

HAWKS OF THE SEAS
BY Willis Rensie
THE HAWK RELATES OF HOW HE FREED THE GALLEY SLAVES - HOW THEY DECIDED TO CHOOSE A LEADER -- THE CREW WAS DIVIDED . . .
THE MEN KNEW BUT ONE LAW OF LEADERSHIP. IT WAS THE SURVIVAL OF THE FITTEST -- THEY CHOSE A POWERFUL FELLOW-- WE WERE GIVEN KNIVES - THE FIRST TO DRAW BLOOD WOULD BE LEADER ...
THE MEN FORMED A CIRCLE ABOUT US...
I REALIZED THAT MY ADVERSARY WAS AN EXPERIENCED FIGHTER. SLOWLY WE CIRCLED EACH OTHER LOOKING FOR AN OPENING...
THEN WITH A CAT-LIKE LEAP--HE LUNGED-I SIDE-STEPPED AND HE WENT SPRAWLING --- THE AUDIENCE SHOUTED THEIR APPROVAL..
ENRAGED, HE SEIZED A BUCKET, FLUNG IT AT ME --- I DUCKED, BUT WENT OFF BALANCE...
HE WAS QUICK TO SEIZE THIS ADVANTAGE, SLOWLY FORCING ME BACK...
WE CLOSED IN A DEATH GRIP!
THEN WITH ALL THE STRENGTH I COULD MUSTER, I WRENCHED FREE AND WOUNDED HIM--- THE CREW ACCEPTED ME AS THEIR LEADER...
AND FROM THEN ON WE BECAME KNOWN AS THE HAWKS OF THE SEAS -- PREYING ON SLAVE SHIPS ONLY.
HAWK, YOU CAN PROVE YOUR INNOCENSE AND RETURN TO SOCIETY--I WILL HELP YOU.
NO- AS A GOVERNOR I WOULD HAVE TO TOLERATE SLAVERY- THAT CAN NEVER BE! AS LONG AS SLAVERY EXISTS I SHALL RE-MAIN THE HAWK.
58.

Hawks of the Seas, page 58. The *Jumbo* run of *Hawks* commenced with page 41 of the 123 page story, for no obvious reason. Worse, when *Jumbo* was reduced in size to match other American comic books, the feature was renamed *The Hawk* and began to run in cut-and-paste form. Eisner had left the company by this time and other artists drew the necessary bridging panels for the reworked version. Even greater indignities befell the series when the artwork was cut apart for a second time and reassembled into an entirely new storyline with new dialogue. After this, the feature passed into the hands of Fiction House staff artist Robert Webb, who continued it for many years.

MEANWHILE, SOMEWHERE IN THE ORIENT.
OUR PLAN WILL SOON BE PUT TO ACTION, COUNT MIROV!
THE PAN-AMERICAN CONFERENCE CONVENES NEXT WEEK.. THE DELE-GATES MUST NOT ATTEND! WE SHALL KILL THEM ALL!
AND WHEN THE SOUTH AMERICAN CONTINENT IS ALL OURS... YOU, MY WISE, BEAUTIFUL ONE, SHALL BE MY EMPRESS!
NO, MIROV, WHEN MY JOB IS DONE, WE PART! I AM IN LOVE WITH SOMEONE ELSE...ONE WHOM I CAN NEVER HOPE TO HAVE... BLACK X!
B-BLACK X!
AH, I SEE YOU BLANCH AT HIS NAME! YES, HE'S THE AMERICAN SECRET AGENT, THE MOST FEARED IN THE WORLD!
TROUBLE NOT YOUR MIND, MASTER. REMEMBER, "THE HEART OF WOMAN IS BUT A MAZE IN WHICH MAN OFT TIMES LOSES HIS WAY!"
WHILE IN NEW YORK.
WELL, BATU, I'M GOING TO MAIL MY RESIGNA-TION. THIS IS THE END OF BLACK X, SECRET AGENT!
DO NOT ACT TOO HASTILY, MASTER!
AS BLACK X LEAVES, INTENT ON FIN-ISHING HIS BUSINESS...
..A SILENT FIGURE COMES IN...

Page 2, *Espionage, Starring Black X* from *Smash Comics* No. 14 (Quality, September, 1940). By this time Will was well embarked on his eccentric approach to page layout. As with the *Uncle Sam Quarterly*, this story was scripted by Will and Lou Fine inked the splash page over his pencils. The rest of the story is all-Eisner.

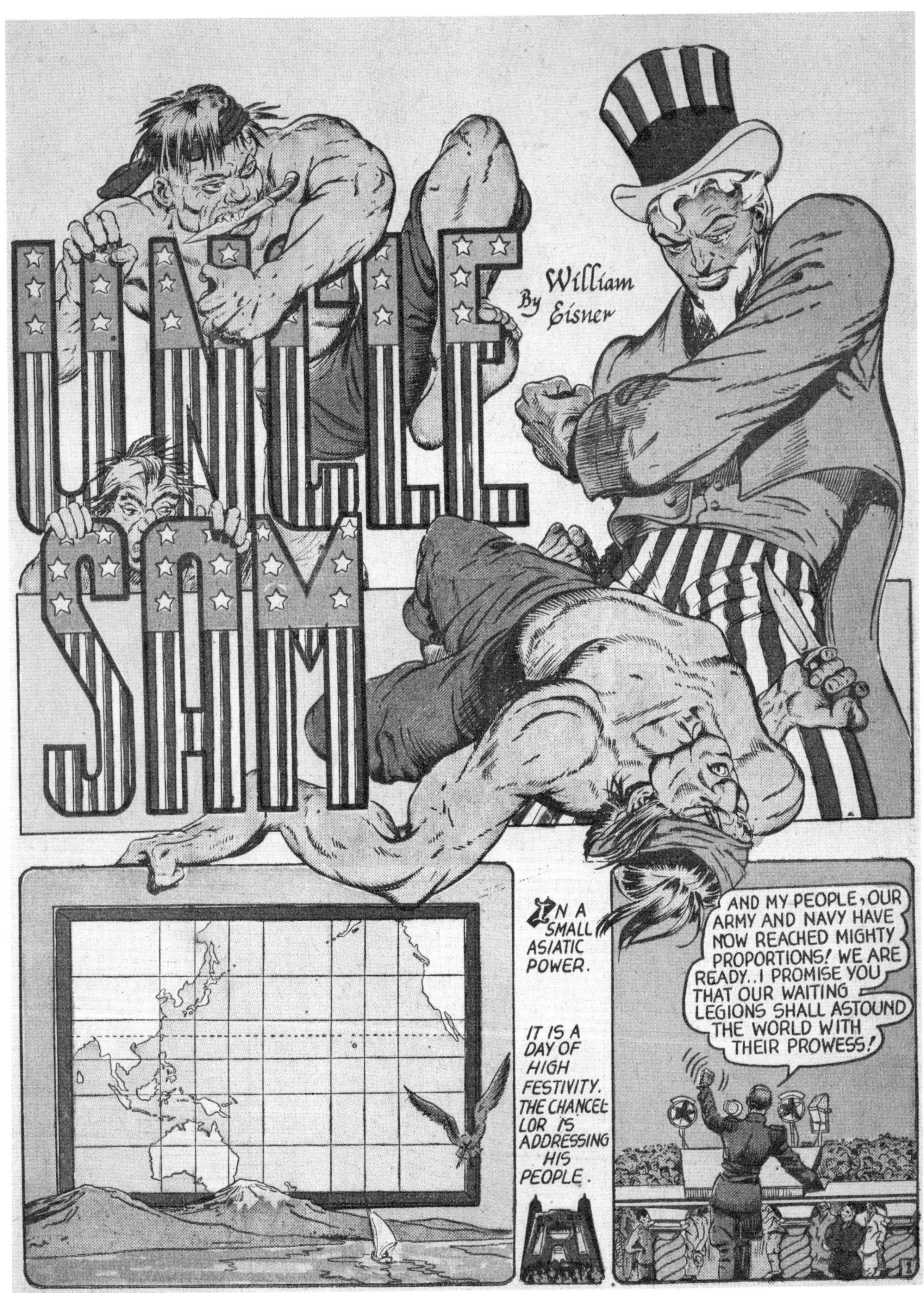
UNCLE SAM
By William Eisner
IN A SMALL ASIATIC POWER.
IT IS A DAY OF HIGH FESTIVITY. THE CHANCEL-LOR IS ADDRESSING HIS PEOPLE.
AND MY PEOPLE, OUR ARMY AND NAVY HAVE NOW REACHED MIGHTY PROPORTIONS! WE ARE READY.. I PROMISE YOU THAT OUR WAITING LEGIONS SHALL ASTOUND THE WORLD WITH THEIR PROWESS!

Splash page, *Uncle Sam* from *National Comics* No. 3 (Quality, September, 1940). This page was another co-operative venture by Eisner and Fine. The script and layouts are Will's, the pencilling Fine's and the inking is Will's. Both men were capable of imitating each other closely at this stage in their careers, although it was usually Will who pencilled and Lou who inked. Typically, the interior artwork for this story is purely Eisner's; the two rarely worked together on the actual story pages.

Forged Faces

The KING of CRIME

The MAN who SOLD his COUNTRY

THE STEEL HELMETS

Four chapter splash pages from *Uncle Sam Quarterly* No. 1 (Quality, Autumn, 1941). Splash pages 1, 2 and 4 are all-Eisner, but no. 3 was inked by Lou Fine over Will's pencils. In a classic display of shop teamwork, the story pages for this issue were drawn by Eisner, Fine, Dave Berg and Chuck Cuidera (often changing from page to page) over a basic script and layouts by Will.

3 The Spirit: 1940-1942

When Will broke up his partnership with Jerry Iger to join Busy Arnold's Quality Comics Group, he was not lured by the prospect of creating, scripting and drawing an endless parade of costumed heroes: he's been doing that for years already. The real appeal was Arnold's proposal to create a comic book newspaper supplement. The *Weekly Comic Book*, as it was first called, was to be printed by Greater Buffalo Press in Buffalo, New York (where Arnold had once been a vice-president) and distributed by the Des Moines Register-Tribune Syndicate. The comic book was 16 pages long, coverless, and boasted that it contained "Three Complete Stories" each issue. From the first, it had a circulation of one and a half million copies; eventually it sold five million copies every week.

Eisner not only put the package together, he created, scripted and drew the lead feature. This was, of course, *The Spirit*, a masked detective-adventurer believed dead by the world, who operated out of his art deco graveyard "laboratory." The series made its debut on June 2, 1940. Within a few weeks, The Spirit (alias Denny Colt) had acquired a young sidekick, Ebony White; a bumbling-but-kindly foil, Police Commissioner Eustace P. Dolan; and an over-eager girlfriend, Dolan's daughter Ellen.

The new comic book also carried two back-up strips, both developed by Eisner but never drawn by him. He drafted at least the first two or three scripts for each, to set the style, but then turned the work over to staff writers. *Lady Luck*, the second feature in the supplement, chronicled the adventures of an Irish-American socialite named Brenda Banks who donned an all-green costume to fight crime and pre-war sabotage. Dick French wrote the series for artists Chuck Mazoujian and Nicholas Viscardi; later Klaus Nordling took on both the script and art chores. He was in turn succeeded by Fred Schwab who had a short run with the feature before it was terminated in late 1946.

Mr. Mystic (his alter-ego, mentioned only once, was "an American named Ken") filled out the comic's last pages. The character was Eisner's reworking of his own earlier feature, *Yarko the Great*. Bob Powell scripted and drew the series until he was drafted into the service. Fred Guardineer then took it on until it was terminated in 1944. It was replaced by an assortment of short funny features like Andre Le Blanc's *Intellectual Amos*, Al Stahl's *Flatfoot Burns*, Bernard Dibble's *Jonesie* and Robert Jenney's *Wendy the Waitress*.

The Spirit was the real star of the *Comic Book Section* (the name was changed shortly after its inception). The strip proved to be exactly the vehicle Eisner needed to take his already daring ideas one step further. From a modest beginning, the series rapidly evolved into one-man virtuoso exploration of the comic medium's potential. Surreal perspectives and lighting effects gave *The Spirit* a compelling aura of mystery. This was surreally augmented by Eisner's seemingly obsessive desire to draw water in all its form, from rain-swept streets to fog-enshrouded, rotting wharves. The graphic close-ups of brutal violence, carefully offset by bouts of slapstick comedy and sexual innuendo, left the reader in a constant state of emotional and aesthetic surprise.

Will Eisner, Nick Viscardi and Bob Powell in the Tudor City studio, 1941.

Ultimately, Eisner began to tamper with the heroic detective-adventure formula itself, developing what comics critic Jules Feiffer called "documentary fables — seemingly authentic when one reads them, but impossible after the fact." One of Feiffer's favorite "documentary fables" was *The Oldest Man In The World*, a daring exercise in colouring as well as a cleverly complex story. It is herewith reprinted exactly as it appeared originally, on October 19, 1941.

COMIC BOOK SECTION

ACTION
Mystery
ADVENTURE

SUNDAY, OCTOBER 19, 1941

THE SPIRIT

BY Will Eisner

Few indeed are the things we little humans know ....but of all in this mysterious world, of only one thing are we certain...even as there was a past so will there be a future...! And so I beg of you, do not scoff at this story....for it is set in a time we know shall surely be...

1,000 years in the future!

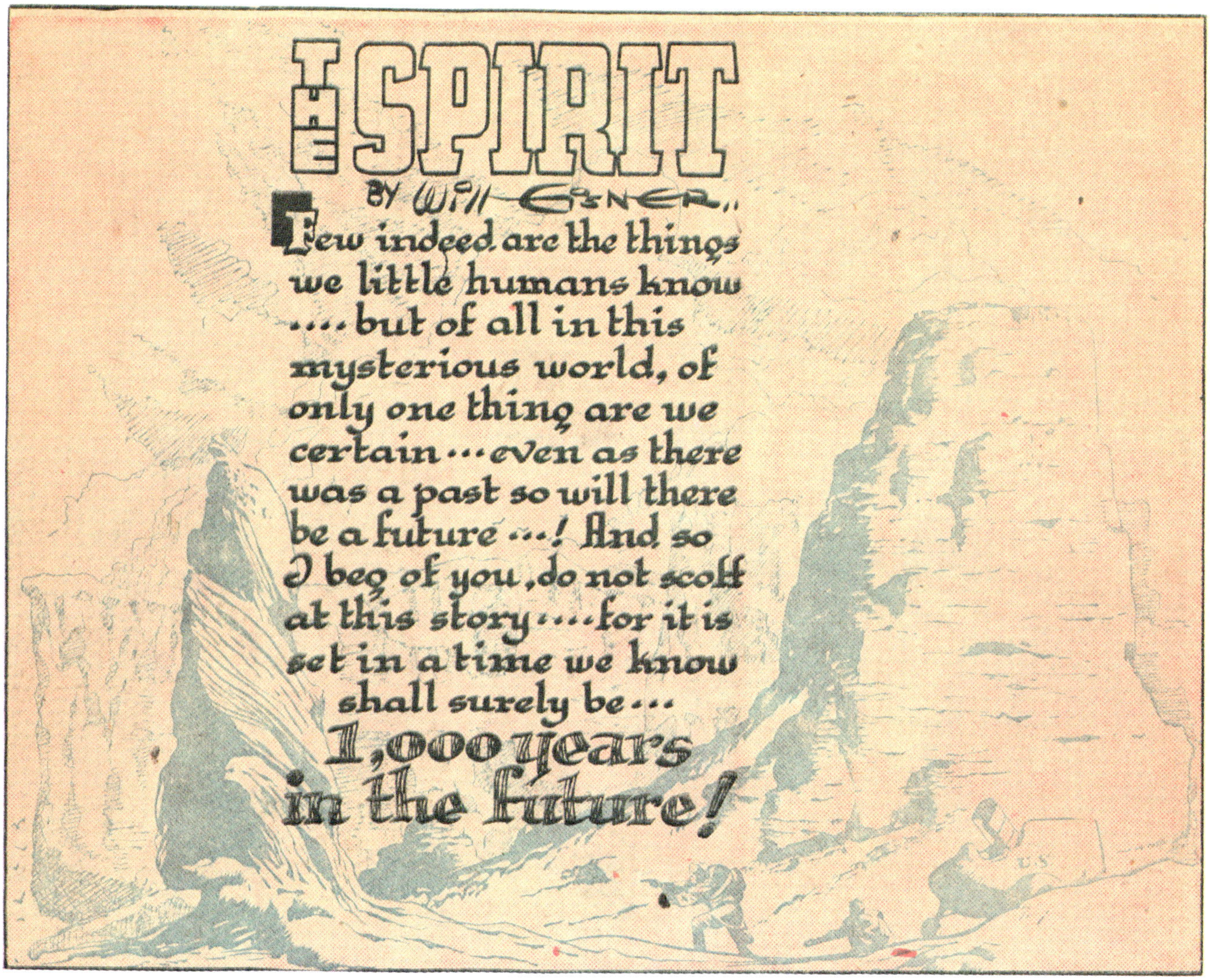

TO BE EXACT, IT IS THE YEAR 2941 A.D. AND HUMANS STILL TROD THE EARTH--- WHY NOT--?? PEOPLE AS WE KNOW THEM CHANGE VERY LITTLE IN 1,000 YEARS---

LET'S LOOK IN UPON TWO ARCHEOLOGISTS DIGGING IN A SECTION THAT WAS ONCE WESTERN UNITED STATES---

AHA---I HAVE FOUND SOMETHING!
INDEED?? WHAT IS IT?

I DON'T KNOW EXACTLY! THEY HAVE NOTHING LIKE THIS IN OUR MUSEUMS! HOWEVER ---ONE COULD FIND ANYTHING IN THIS DESOLATE SECTION OF THE COUNTRY!
IT IS MADE OF THAT SUBSTANCE CALLED PAPER---- THAT MUCH IS CLEAR!

YOU ARE CORRECT--- AND THERE IS WRITING-- WITH PICTURES IN COLOR--- AH--SEE? IT IS PRINTED!!
YES--AMAZING WHAT THOSE PEOPLE DID WITH SUCH CRUDE INSTRUMENTS. I WONDER WHAT DATE IT IS?

IT SAYS---1941!! CAN YOU IMAGINE? ---1000 YEARS AGO!! THIS IS A RARE FIND!!
STRANGE SUCH A FRAGILE PIECE OF PAPER PRESERVED SO LONG!!

AH, I SEE NOW! THE SAP OF THIS TREE RAN OVER IT AND PRESERVED IT--A COINCIDENCE OF NATURE!!
HANDLE IT CAREFULLY ---LET'S READ WHAT IT SAYS!

"THE SPIRIT"-- BY--HMM, CAN'T MAKE OUT THE AUTHOR'S NAME!

--DOESN'T MATTER--- AH--SEE THE TITLE-- "THE OLDEST MAN IN THE WORLD"---

THE SUNDAY Herald Gazette

SUNDAY, OCT. 19, 1941

ACTION Mystery ADVENTURE

COMIC BOOK SECTION

The Spirit BY Will Eisner

The Oldest Man in the World

10-19

Reg. U. S. Pat. Off.

Distributed by Register and Tribune Syndicate

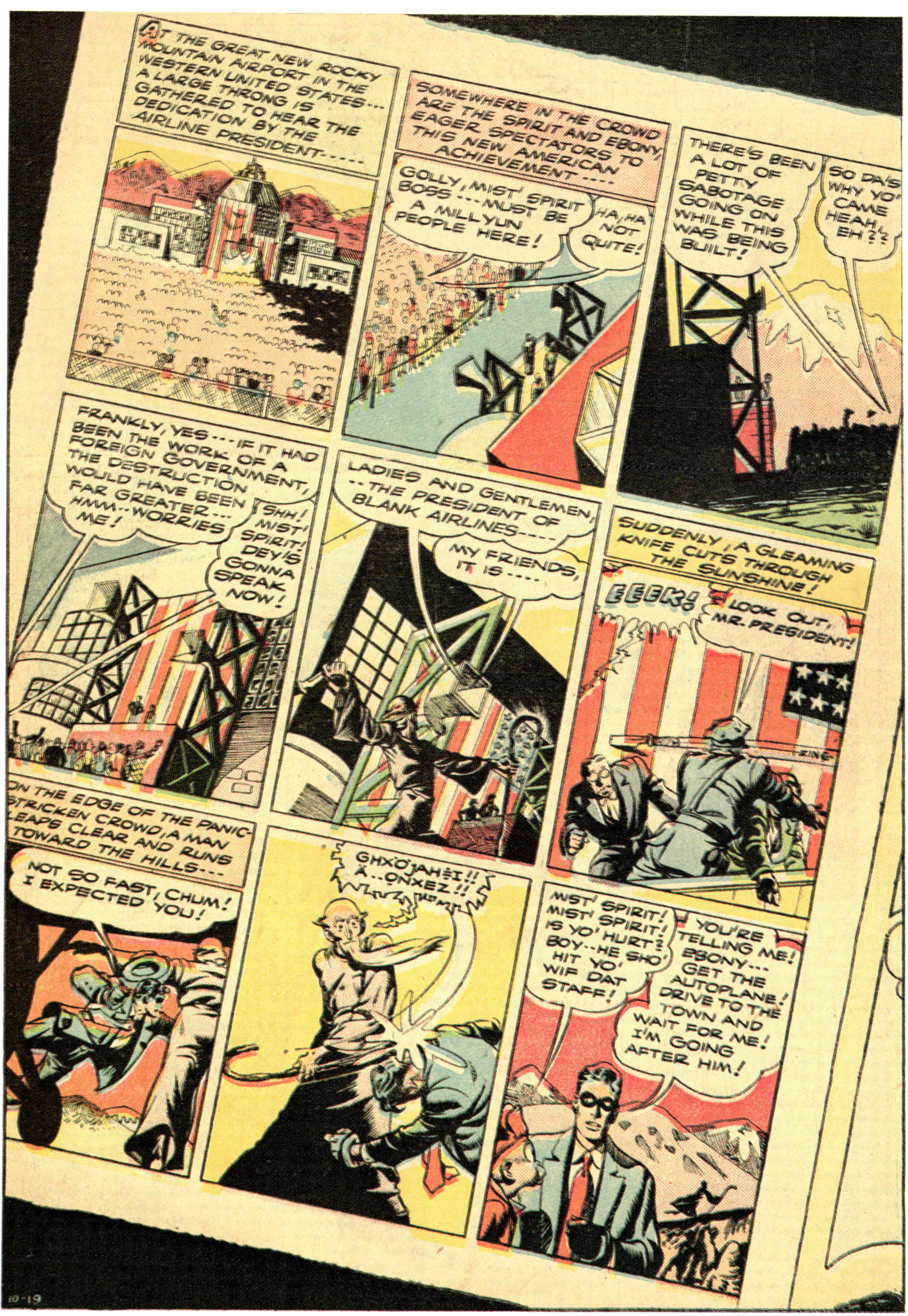
AT THE GREAT NEW ROCKY MOUNTAIN AIRPORT IN THE WESTERN UNITED STATES--- A LARGE THRONG IS GATHERED TO HEAR THE DEDICATION BY THE AIRLINE PRESIDENT-----
SOMEWHERE IN THE CROWD ARE THE SPIRIT AND EBONY, EAGER SPECTATORS TO THIS NEW AMERICAN ACHIEVEMENT ----
GOLLY, MIST' SPIRIT BOSS---MUST BE A MILLYUN PEOPLE HERE!
HA, HA NOT QUITE!
THERE'S BEEN A LOT OF PETTY SABOTAGE GOING ON WHILE THIS WAS BEING BUILT!
SO DAT'S WHY YO' CAME HEAH, EH??
FRANKLY, YES---IF IT HAD BEEN THE WORK OF A FOREIGN GOVERNMENT, THE DESTRUCTION WOULD HAVE BEEN FAR GREATER... HMM--WORRIES ME!
SHH! MIST' SPIRIT! DEY'S GONNA SPEAK NOW!
LADIES AND GENTLEMEN, --THE PRESIDENT OF BLANK AIRLINES----
MY FRIENDS, IT IS----
SUDDENLY, A GLEAMING KNIFE CUTS THROUGH THE SUNSHINE!
EEEK!
LOOK OUT, MR. PRESIDENT!
ON THE EDGE OF THE PANIC-STRICKEN CROWD, A MAN LEAPS CLEAR AND RUNS TOWARD THE HILLS---
NOT SO FAST, CHUM! I EXPECTED YOU!
MIST' SPIRIT! MIST' SPIRIT! IS YO' HURT? BOY--HE SHO' HIT YO' WIF DAT STAFF!
YOU'RE TELLING ME! EBONY--- GET THE AUTOPLANE! DRIVE TO THE TOWN AND WAIT FOR ME! I'M GOING AFTER HIM!
10-19

AN INSTANT LATER, THE SPIRIT IS IN PURSUIT....
QUEER LOOKING DUCK ..AND HIS LANGUAGE ..LIKE NOTHING EARTHLY...
AH..THERE HE GOES!
..BUT MEANWHILE FAR BELOW, STATE TROOPERS ARE ON THE TRAIL....
LOOK, SERGEANT!! THERE HE GOES!
GIVE ME A RIFLE!
GOT HIM!! LET'S GO GET HIM!
WHEW..WHAT A CLIMB... HEY..HE'S GONE!!
BUT I'M SURE I SAW HIM FALL!!
MUST HAVE CRAWLED OFF..LOOKED LIKE ONE O' THESE MOUNTAINEER FOLK.. AND IF I KNOW THEM WE'LL NOT FIND HIM TODAY!
I HATE TO DEPRIVE THE POLICE OF THEIR QUARRY, BUT THERE'S A LOT MORE BEHIND THIS THAN THEY THINK, ..EH, OLD TIMER? HERE..HAVE A DRINK!! WHEW! LOOKS LIKE THAT BULLET ENTERED YOUR HEART... BEFORE YOU DIE, TELL ME, WHY DID YOU...
I DIE? THUNDEROUS BLASPHEMY IN EMPTY CHASMS. NO! TEN MILLION TIMES NO!!! I AM AGELESS! I SHALL LIVE FOREVER!!
??
IT'S BEGINNING TO RAIN... COME UNDER THIS ROCK! YOU'RE ....
NO, NO! I SHOUT FROM THE BOTTOMLESS VALLEYS!! I CANNOT DIE! I WILL LIVE FOREVER!!

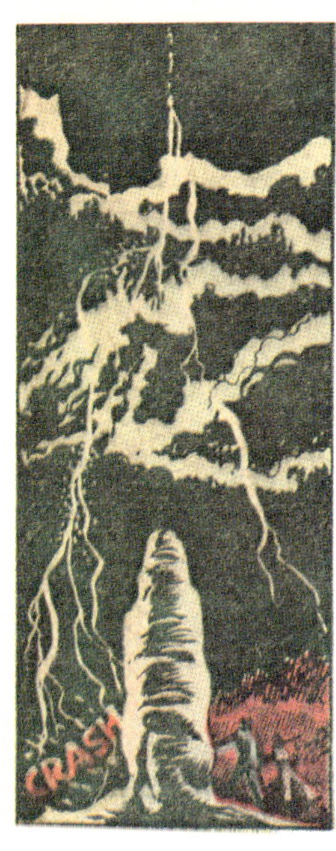
CRASH

GOOD GRAVY! A LIGHTNING STORM! YOU'RE MAD! ARE YOU COMING PEACEFULLY OR--
FOOL! FOOL! FATHOM-LESS FOOL!! CRUMBLING GORGES AND TREMBLING EAR-R-TH!! --MUST I PROVE IT?

LOOK!...LITTLE ANT OF THE EARTH--SEE--MY WOUND HAS STOPPED BLEEDING! IT IS HEALED!

GOOD GRAVY! HE'S RIGHT!!

WHO ARE YOU? WHAT IS YOUR NAME? WHY ARE YOU HERE?
WHO-- WHAT-- WHY-- A THUNDERCLAP IN THE VALLEY OF THE DEAD--- HE CONFOUNDS ME!

HEE---HA HA HA HA HA HA

YOU ARE A BRAVE MAN... ANY OTHER WOULD QUAIL BEFORE MY WRATH...SO I WILL TELL YOU WHAT NO LIVING MAN HAS HEARD! EONS AGO---BEFORE THE BIRTH OF TIME....I WAS BANISHED FROM THE PALE OF MEN! I WAS SENTENCED TO LIVE FOREVER.... FOR A CRIME SO GREAT THAT THE TINY FISHES ON THE OCEAN FLOOR RECOILED WITH SHAME!

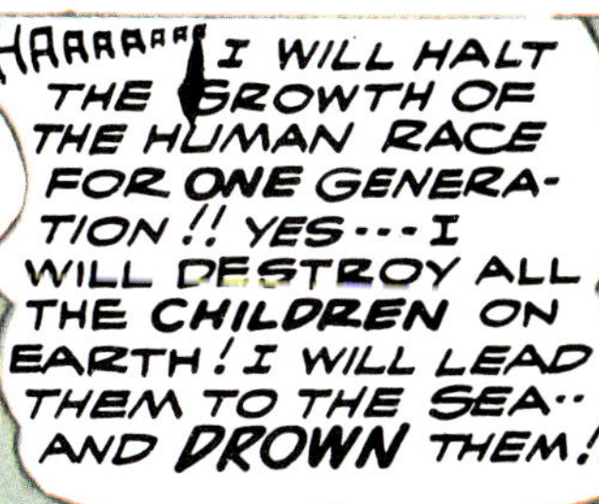
BUT WHY DID YOU TRY TO KILL THE PRESIDENT?
BECAUSE I WISH TO STOP THE GROWTH OF THE HUMAN RACE! THERE ARE TOO MANY PEOPLE ON EARTH!! THEY ARE CROWDING ME OFF THE SURFACE... SOON CITIES WILL BE ALL OVER AND I WILL HAVE NO WILD COUNTRY TO HIDE IN!

HAAAAAA! I WILL HALT THE GROWTH OF THE HUMAN RACE FOR ONE GENERATION!! YES---I WILL DESTROY ALL THE CHILDREN ON EARTH! I WILL LEAD THEM TO THE SEA-- AND DROWN THEM!!

AND SO, THE NEXT MORNING, JUST AFTER DAWN--THE ECHO OF CHILDREN'S LAUGHTER BOUNCES ACROSS THE VALLEYS TO THE PLAINS BELOW, AWAKENING THE STARTLED TOWNSPEOPLE...

LOOK! A PARADE OF CHILDREN!

BIG CHILDREN...LITTLE CHILDREN--SKIPPING, SCURRYING, SMILING, SINGING, STUMBLING IN THE WAKE OF THE OLD PIPER..... AS THEY PASS THROUGH THE TOWN, MORE CHILDREN JOIN THE RANKS ....LIKE LITTLE FRESHETS SWALLOWED BY A SWOLLEN STREAM....

...THROUGH TOWN AFTER TOWN THEY PASS--ALWAYS IT IS THE SAME ----

TOMMY TOMMY COME BACK!!
NO USE, MARY! I CAN'T STOP HIM!
STOP THEM! OH DEAR HEAVEN, STOP THEM!!

--UP THROUGH THE PASSES OF THE ROCKY MOUNTAINS--

--AND DOWN THE OTHER SIDE----NO LONGER A STREAM, BUT A MIGHTY TORRENT OF CHILDREN....

--UNTIL AT LAST THEY HALT AT THE BRINK OF A HIGH CLIFF, AGAINST WHOSE BASE THE ANGRY, HUNGRY SEA HURLS ITSELF WITH SAVAGE FURY!

But.... OVERHEAD, LIKE A HAWK...THE SPIRIT CIRCLES IN HIS AUTOPLANE.... WATCHING--WAITING....

GOLLY--MUST BE A MILLION OF 'EM!! LOOKS LIKE DEY'S GONNA JUMP INTO THE SEA!!
THEY WILL UNLESS-- EBONY! I'VE DECIDED...

EBONY--I'VE LIVED A FULL LIFE--I'VE BEEN HAPPY AND BEEN SAD--I THINK NOW'S THE TIME FOR ME TO DIE! NOW, WHEN MY DEATH WILL SERVE A PURPOSE!
MIST' SPIRIT!! WHAT IS YO' SAYIN! IS YO' TETCHED?

NO, EBONY! I'M SANE.. THERE'S ONLY ONE WAY TO STOP HIM! I MUST JUMP INTO THE SEA--AND TAKE HIM WITH ME! THAT IS THE ONLY SURE WAY TO SAVE THOSE CHILDREN!
SOB
NO NO
GOLLY-- PLEASE, MIST' SPIRIT!!

AND AS THE AUTOPLANE SWOOPS LOW----
NO, MIST' SPIRIT---NO PLEASE! WHAT IS AH GONNA DO?

FOR A MOMENT BOTH MEN LINGER ON THE EDGE--STRUGGLING WITH THE SAVAGE ABANDON OF MEN WHO FEAR NO DEATH!

SMASHING METEORS! CRUSHING WORLDS!!
YOU WILL NOT-- YOU DARE NOT!! ÖAFNEX!!

AH JES' GOTTA-- AH JES' GOTTA SAVE HIM!

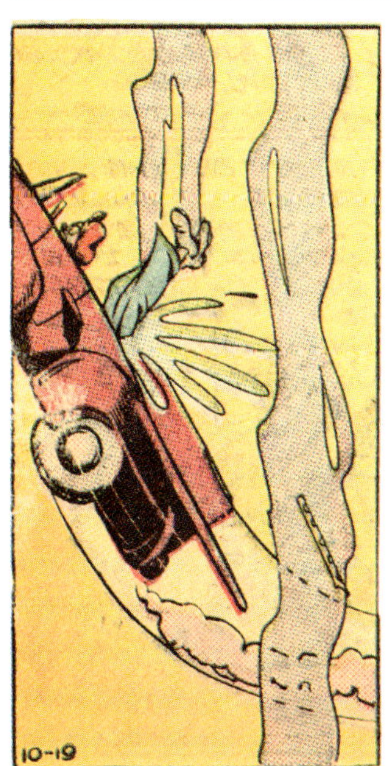
10-19

THANK HEBEN! AH DONE IT--AH DONE IT!!

WHILE FAR BELOW, THE SEA SUCKS A NEW VICTIM, DOWN, DOWN INTO HER CAVERNOUS DEPTHS---

--AND AS THE AUTOPLANE HEADS BACK TO WILDWOOD, THE CHILDREN CAN BE SEEN DIMLY IN THE DISTANCE, RETURNING TO HOME AND LOVED ONES----

I'M GLAD THE SPIRIT WAS SAVED! HE MUST HAVE BEEN A GREAT MAN!
YES--I CAN BELIEVE THAT---BUT THAT OLDEST MAN IN THE WORLD----

I CANNOT BELIEVE THAT! HE WAS A CHARLATAN-- A FAKE--AND THE SPIRIT WAS A FOOL TO RISK HIS LIFE....

I DON'T KNOW--- PEOPLE IN THOSE DAYS HAD QUAINT BELIEFS---
OH!

UGH!

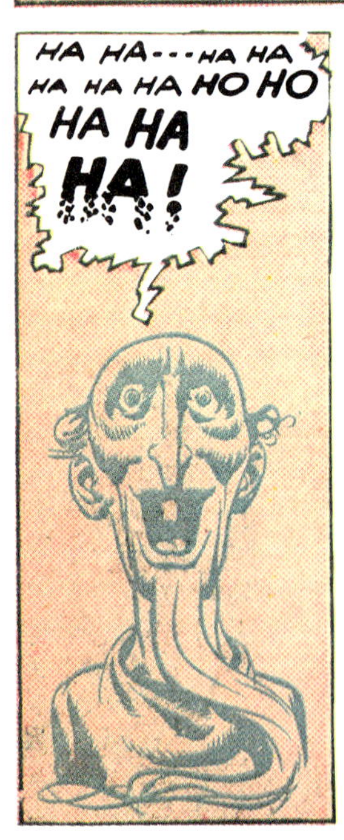
HA HA---HA HA HA HA HA HO HO HA HA HA!

CRASHING THUNDER IN THE CAVES OF THE DEAF!

FROM THE DESOLATE WASTES OF ABANDONED WILDWOOD CEMETERY WHERE HE WAS MISTAKENLY BURIED, THE SPIRIT, IN REALITY DENNY COLT, SMASHES CRIME IN A NEVER-ENDING WAR AGAINST THE ENEMIES OF SOCIETY.
The
SPIRIT
BY
Will Eisner

Spirit splash page, January 12, 1941 (*The Silk District Beat*). The "symbolic" splash page at its best — a giant Spirit toys with tiny criminals against the ominous skyline of the city.

THE Spirit
BY Will Eisner

Spirit splash page, December 1, 1940 (*At The Prom*).

THE SPIRIT
DENNY COLT IS, IN REALITY, NOT DEAD AS THE WORLD BELIEVES.. INSTEAD, AS THE SPIRIT HE WAGES A SINGLE HANDED WAR ON CRIME....
BY Will Eisner

Spirit splash page, December 8, 1940 (*The Haunted House*).

TO CENTRAL CITY EACH YEAR COME THOUSANDS OF IMMIGRANTS SEEKING REFUGE IN THE MELTING POT THAT IS AMERICA, AND BRINGING WITH THEM THE GOOD AND THE EVIL OF A WORLD IN FLAMES ... FOR EVIL KNOWS NO BOUNDRIES AND TRAVELS SWIFTEST WITH WICKED MEN ... BUT LET THEM BEWARE, FOR TO THE NORTH LIES WILDWOOD CEMETERY WHERE LIVES CRIME'S MIGHTIEST FOE ...
BY Will Eisner
THE SPIRIT
HA-HA-HA! LET THE SPIRIT BEWARE OF THE WRATH OF THE BLACK BOW!!

Spirit splash page, January 5, 1941 (*The Black Bow*).

BY Will Eisner
HALLOWE'EN...
...A TIME OF WITCHES, GOBLINS AND SKELETONS .....BUT WAIT--IT IS NOT YET NIGHT--IT IS THE TIME WHEN ALL THE WORLD GROWS SILENT (IN MOURNING FOR THE DYING DAY, NO DOUBT)--WHEN THE SKY DARKENS AND FROM THE SHADOWS OF THE EARTH STEPS DUSK--THE SILENT HERALD OF THE NIGHT!!
THE SPIRIT
10-26

Spirit splash page, October 26, 1941 (*Hallowe'en Dusk*).

IN THE FEDERAL PENITENTIARY NEAR CENTRAL CITY... THE PRISON IS A GREY, SLEEPING HULK... ONLY ONE LIGHT CASTS AN EERIE GLEAM OUT INTO THE FOG... THE CELL OF A CONDEMNED MAN IN THE DEATH HOUSE....
WHAT TIME IS IT, GUARD?
9:45
TWO HOURS AND FIFTEEN MINUTES TO LIVE!! @#!!**!
...AND DEEP IN CENTRAL CITY'S SLUMS, ANOTHER WINDOW IS LIT IN THE NIGHT....
H MM... 9:45... JUST TWO HOURS AND FIFTEEN MINUTES MORE AND LITTLE PETE GETS IT!
WHO'S THERE?
TAKE IT EASY, MONKS... IT'S US... I GOT A COUPLA BOYS WID ME!
TORONTO PHIL... DENVER SAM.. WEEPY WILLIE.. AND SOUP McCANN... MEET D'BOSS, MONKS MALLON!
H'YA
'LO
UGH!
AAH HAAH!
HMM.. I HOPE YOU GUYS ARE AS TOUGH AS Y'R SUPPOSED TO BE, BECAUSE THE GUY Y'R GONNA RUB OUT IS THE SPIRIT!!

Page 2, *The Spirit*, November 2, 1941 (*The Confession of Monks Mallon*). A good example of Eisner's story-telling techniques, using parallel visual development of two interwoven plots enhanced by unexpected, mood-setting angle shots.

"THE SPIRIT" OF '41

BANG!
IT WOULD THOROUGHLY FRIGHTEN YOU GOOD CITIZENS TO REALLY KNOW WHAT THINGS GO ON BENEATH THE SILENCE IN CENTRAL CITY AFTER DARK....FOR INSTANCE.....
NOW WHAT!?...WE CAN'T REMAIN HERE! WE MUST GO!
EXACTLY!! WE'RE GOING TO YOUR OFFICE...AT POLICE HEADQUARTERS!!
MIST' SPIRIT BOSS...AS YO' CHIEF ASSISTANT AH FEELS IT MAH BOUNDEN DUTY TO ACCOMPANY YO' ON ALL DANGEROUS MISSIONS....
?
COMMISSIONER DOLAN!! GOOD HEAVENS!! YOU'VE KILLED HIM!!
THE SPIRIT!! WHAT ARE YOU DOING HERE?!!

WILL EISNER AND "THE SPIRIT"
. . . Plutarch got in the baloon.

By NORMAN ABBOTT

The Spirit's lithe body pivoted suddenly like a thing of finely tempered steel. His right fist shot out (The Spirit shows a regrettable tendency to lead with his right) and crashed into the leering, ugly face before him. The man dropped like a felled ox. As the rest of the evil gang surged forward, The Spirit hurled them aside and plunged through the window. In the darkened streets of the sleeping city . . .

* * *

A mild young man with intelligent eyes, a fondness for Plutarch, and a deep interest in the academicians among painters, puts down his brush and wishes that he could find time to ask a girl for a date. The rest of his staff has long gone and it's after midnight and Will Eisner is winding up another 18-hour day in his New York studio. The Spirit, he reflects, leads a tolerably active life and yet even he gets more rest than the poor guy who invented him.

Eisner is 24. In the past five years he has converted hogsheads of India ink into thrills and set down, on drawing paper, prodigious quantities of violent adventure. And now that The Spirit is to perform in a daily strip (it starts today in The Record) instead of just once a week in the Sunday Record's comic book, Eisner is beginning to wonder if he really needs to devote six hours in each day just to eating and sleeping and loafing.

Has Big Plans

Curiously, though, he is unwearied by the requirements of his brawny baby. His plans for The Spirit, and for the entire field of comic-strip adventure, are sufficiently ambitious to absorb all the enthusiasm of even a studious and gifted young man who once believed an artist was a man who went off from the world and worked slowly and lovingly in oils.

The comic strip, he explains, is no longer a comic strip but, in reality, an illustrated novel. It is new and raw in form just now, but material for limitless intelligent development. And eventually and inevitably it will be a legitimate medium for the best of writers and artists. It is already the embryo - Eisner apologizes a little for the trite phrase - of a new art form. And he believes in it and will stay with it proudly, and without apologies. Even now, with all his love of the classical painters, he finds it a satisfactory form of self-expression.

Eisner, a New Yorker by birth, was graduated from the DeWitt Clinton High School with a scholarship in the Art Students League. His talent had to earn him a living, however, and he moved swiftly from classes into professional jobs: Art editor and assistant art editor of a variety of trade and club magazines. In the winter of 1936-37 the astonishing boom in newsstand comic magazines attracted him. He opened a studio and announced to publishers that he was prepared to supply adventure in endless amounts.

Trade Boomed

From the beginning, his trade boomed. In two and a half years he had a staff of 20 at work and was planning, drawing and supervising the complete contents of 15 comic books a month. Some of his strips were being syndicated in Latin America and American kids were worrying their parents into fits by their preoccupation with such items as "Espionage," "The Doll Man," "Uncle Sam," "The Black Condor," and the like.

"In those days anything went," Eisner explains. "It was like the early days of the movies. They bought anything. But it has changed unbelievably now. I was astonished to learn how high the average intelligence rate of children is. It's higher than it ever was, I think. It is impossible to write down to them. They want action, naturally, but they demand plausibility, too. It is possible to gauge a strip for adults and children alike, because the young mind is keen enough to understand the plots."

Careful Planning

The Spirit was planned that way. About a year and a half ago Eisner was associated with E. M. Arnold, publisher of the nine magazines which comprise the Quality Comic Group, when they discussed a weekly supplement to be distributed through newspapers. Eisner, familiar with all the comic formulae by then, plotted The Spirit as carefully as any novel.

"The rest was a matter of environment and plot. I decided definitely against scenes of overpowering gruesomeness and the kind of sexiness which has no place in a strip children will read. I wanted to keep down killings and bloodshed. When I was finished, I had The Spirit in its first form. It has developed as the people in it become real to me."

A good deal of unexpected background goes into the strip. Most of it is a result of Eisner's casual reading. He has a passion for history and biography, and although he doesn't read in conscious search of material for his job, ideas keep popping out. He has drawn from Plutarch, biographies of Napoleon and even Machiavelli's "The Prince." He quoted Machiavelli in a baloon caption once and was delighted to receive letters from college professors and Judges saying that it sounded familiar, and was it his own phrase or had he read it somewhere? He wrote back, giving the source.

Proud of Letters

He is proud of letters like that—and he gets a number from people who might ordinarily be aloof from comic strips—but he is prouder of the fact that the parents' and church leagues which object to a number of bloodier comics have no fault to find with his. Clergymen and club leaders have told him they find The Spirit unobjectionable; teachers have confessed they like it.

"First," he said, "I decided my leading figure wouldn't be what we call a costume character—one of the unreal heroes who wears a strange cloak or suit and does impossible things. I didn't believe children would maintain interest in someone they couldn't imagine meeting on the street. When I decided upon The Spirit, I worked from the inside out, you might say.

"That is, I thought first of his personality—the kind of a man he was to be, how he would look at problems, how he would feel about life, the sort of mind he would have. When that was worked out, I didn't have to imagine him as a person. I began to see him. Handsome, obviously, and powerfully built, but not one of those impossibly big, thick-legged brutes. He was to be the kind of man a child could conceive of seeing on the street.

Mask a Fillip

"Then I gave him a mask, as a sort of fillip to his personality. And he had to be on the side of the law, of course, but I believed it would be better if he worked a little outside of the law. In that way he acquires some of the sympathy most of us feel for adventurers who are absolutely on their own. And for a necessary tie-up with the regular police, I gave him Commissioner Dolan. Then, we needed humor, hence Ebony, and, of course, there had to be a girl. The kind of girl, pretty and clean-cut and brave, whom a man like The Spirit would like."

Most of Eisner's other work has been given up because of his concentration on The Spirit, although he still plans and draws a great deal of "Mr. Mystic" and "Lady Luck," the other stories which appear in The Spirit Comic Book. He keeps a staff of only 10 now. They do the lettering, research and part of the drawing, although the plotting and planning of episodes, and the creation of key characters and scenes, is still exclusively his job.

For recreation, he tries to get down into Georgia for quail shooting at least once or twice a year, fishes when he can, and plays all the tennis a man can get in on a seven-day week. He rides the subways and prowls New York streets occasionally, looking for characters he can insert later into The Spirit's adventures. But mostly, he thinks about his fast-growing husky and his future. (The Spirit's future, that is; Eisner's ought to be pretty well assured.)

Some day, he believes, the comic strip technique will even find a place in the schools. He'd like that. And it would manifestly be all right with the kids.

On Monday, October 13, 1941, the daily *Spirit* comic strip opened in the Philadelphia *Record* with the usual flurry of publicity. The article at left contains a photo of Eisner taken at the office of the *Record*, as well as panels from the first two dailies. Will can be seen inking a large head of *The Spirit*. Above is an unpublished photo taken minutes after the first one. On the left is Eisner's business partner, Busy Arnold. The man pretending to threaten Will with a yardstick is the comics feature editor for the *Record*. His full name is unknown, but his nickname is evidently "Gup," as can be seen in the inscription Eisner has added to the now-complete drawing. "To Gup," it reads, "With Best Wishes, Will Eisner." Busy Arnold is holding a large manilla envelope in his hands, which suggests that the drawing was brought from New York City in pencilled form with the intention of using it as a prop in the published photo.

THE SPIRIT
(Now! Daily and Sunday: THE SPIRIT—America's Crime Smasher No. 1)
By Will Eisner
IT WOULD THOROUGHLY FRIGHTEN YOU GOOD CITIZENS TO REALLY KNOW WHAT THINGS GO ON BENEATH THE SILENCE IN CENTRAL CITY AFTER DARK....FOR INSTANCE.....
BANG!
CLICK
COMMISSIONER DOLAN!! GOOD HEAVENS!! YOU'VE KILLED HIM!!
THE SPIRIT!! WHAT ARE YOU DOING HERE?!!

The first *Spirit* daily, October 13, 1941.

THE SPIRIT

By Will Eisner

ANTED
wears blue gloves
never carries a gun
has an airplane
seen in company of Ellen Dolan
address unknown
THE SPIRIT
has little assistant named Ebony
wears cap... short red jacket buttons
helps police sometimes
© 1941 The Register and Tribune Syndicate

VELLY SAD, MASTAH SPHINX ---- HAVE MUCH OF WHAT SPIRIT DO, BUT LITTLE OF WHO HE IS!!!

IF WE ARE TO COLLECK MILLION DOLLAH WHICH SQUIRE SAMPSON LEAVE TO MEN WHO UNMASK SPIRIT, WE MUST GET INFORMATION FROM SPIRIT HEESELF !!

OF COURSE TORTURE MAY BE NECESSARY, BUT ---- MONEY WOULD NOT BE REFUSED IF US PRESENT SPIRIT HEESELF --- DEAD!!!

THE SPIRIT

By Will Eisner

I AM MISS DOLLY DEVERE, THE SINGER ---- I GOT A NOTE FROM A GUY NAMED THE SPHINX --- I --

SSHH!! PLEASE GLAB SEAT --- MASTAH WRITE SONG!!

Y'MEAN YOUR BOSS IS A SONG WRITER ?!!
NOT QUITE!! WE WISH YOU TO SING SONG IN NIGHT CLUB ---- SO SPIRIT HEAR ABOUT IT -- COME TO SEE ---- HEE--HEE ---- WE COTCH HIM!!!

Y'MEAN YOU GUYS ARE GONNA TRY TO TO COLLECT THAT MONEY SQUIRE LEFT TO ANYONE WHO CAN FIND OUT WHO THE SPIRIT IS?
YES!!
© 1941 The Register and Tribune Syndicate

BOYS --- YOU'VE GOT A PARTNER ---- WHERE DO WE GO FROM HERE? I'M GAME FOR ANYTHING!!

Spirit dailies, December 10 and 11, 1941.

This photo of Will, taken in his Tudor City studio in October, 1941, clearly shows him inking the above two *Spirit* dailies.

THE SPIRIT

By Will Eisner

HE WILL DIE OF MY BITE BEFORE LONG!! NOW, MASTAH, WE MUST GO TO LAWYER'S OFFICE ... REVEAL WHO SPIRIT IS AND COLLECT MILLION DOLLAH .... HEE, HEE, HEE!!!

THE SPIRIT

By Will Eisner

CODGER, DODGER!! COME HERE AT ONCE!!
CODGER DODGER AND SPARROW ATTORNEYS

THE LITTLE MAN, KAIBASH, JUST PHONED! HE SAID FOR US TO HAVE THE MILLION DOLLARS READY IN 1,000 DOLLAR BILLS .... THEY KNOW WHO THE SPIRIT IS!! AND ACCORDING TO SQUIRE SAMPSON'S WILL WE MUST PAY IT OUT TO THEM!!

HEE, HEE, HEE!! WITH MY SHARE OF THE MONEY, MASTAH, I WILL BUY MYSELF A PALACE IN INDIA WEETH 1000 LOVELY WIFES!!

MEANWHILE ....
GH ... THAT BITE KAIBASH GAVE ME ... I'M POISONED!! ... BUT I MUST STOP THEM ... I MUST ....

THE SPIRIT

By Will Eisner

SQUIRE SAMPSON LEAVES MILLION TO PERSON WHO UNMASKS THE SPIRIT!

THE SPIRIT

By Will Eisner

WELL, AT LAST THE MOMENT HAS ARRIVED ... THE SPHINX AND KAIBASH ARE COMING TO REVEAL THE SPIRIT'S TRUE IDENTITY!!
AND WE MUST PAY THEM ONE MILLION DOLLARS ACCORDING TO SQUIRE SAMPSON'S WILL ... GEE!! I WISH SOME OF THIS WAS LEFT TO ME!!

AND SOMEWHERE .....
GOT TO STOP 'EM ...

WHILE ....
HULLY UP, MAHSTA SPHINX ... MILLION DOLLAH ALMOST IN GLASP ... HEE HEE .. SPIRIT DEAD BY NOW!!
HEE HEE !!
WHY, IF IT ISN'T MY OLD PALS, SPHINX AND KAIBASH!!

Spirit dailies, January 1, 2, 3 and 5, 1941. The daily plotline had no continuity with the Sunday *Spirit* stories (one of which ran on January 4th).

Follow THE SPIRIT *Daily* in The Record

COMIC BOOK SECTION

RECORD
PHILADELPHIA

SUNDAY, MAY 3, 1942

THE SPIRIT
By Will Eisner

Where's the Spirit? The Editor

Deadline, Spirit story due..

Eisner, you are late!! The Editor

Spirit splash page, May 3, 1942 (Self Portrait). This page was pencilled by Will and inked by Lou Fine. It is an accurate representation of Eisner at his drawing board in Quality's Tudor City studio. His induction into the Army led him to hire Fine as a ghost artist for the duration of the war.

The War Years: 1942-1945

"I was sitting at my desk in Tudor City, inking a *Spirit* page. The radio was on — a Philharmonic broadcast, I believe. I had just eaten a sandwich of pot roast and mayonnaise on rye, which my mother had made for me that morning. The announcer interrupted the program to say that Pearl Harbor had been bombed. I knew it was all over then; I'd be drafted for sure. I'd stalled off my draft board as long as I could, but no more.

"I dipped my brush, whittled it on the side of my desk and went back to stroking in ink on the *Spirit* page which was due the next day."

Eisner was inducted in May, 1942. After a short time at Camp Dix, New Jersey, he was shipped to Aberdeen Proving Ground with the Ordnance Department. Once in Maryland, he began to produce editorial cartoons and a weekly humour strip for the camp newspaper, *The Flaming Bomb.* Promoted to the rank of corporal, he competed in a contest and won the right to paint a series of posters which were displayed on Army bases to encourage the idea of preventive maintenance of vehicles and weapons.

Eventually Eisner made the rank of Chief Warrant Officer and was transferred to the Pentagon. There he provided articles and illustrations for a variety of Army publications, including *Firepower* ("The Ordnance Man's Journal") and *Army Motors* ("The Magazine of Preventive Maintenance").

Eisner at target practice in the Army, circa 1942.

The Washington Post

Saturday, September 23, 1944

Not You, Fella!

Pvt. Joe Dope, Reverse Hero, Is a 'Pixie'

By Anne Hagner

Pvt. Joe Dope is the Army's worst mechanic, but Ordnance Department officers, who love him for his faults, will not permit him to have any know-how. For from Joe Dope, flesh-and-blood soldiers learn valuable lessons in preventive maintenance.

Joe, hero in reverse of 50-odd posters and a comic strip all his own, has stripped more gears and jammed more guns than any yardbird in the service. His chubby cheeks and twin-tombstone teeth are visible in every machine shop from Aberdeen (Md.) Proving Ground to the China-Burma-India theater, and commanding officers continue to demand more Joe Dopes—all on paper, of course.

Private Dope was born—well, drafted—two years ago when Maj. Gen. L. H. Campbell, jr., chief of ordnance, and Col. L. A. Codd decided that there should be a "horrible example" before the eyes of maintenance men.

At that point, a brand new private at Aberdeen was earning a reputation for being pretty handy with a drawing brush, and Ordnance officers discovered that he was Will Eisner, creator of "The Spirit" which was becoming firmly entrenched as a Nation-wide comic strip here.

To Eisner was given the job of developing "Pvt. Joe Dope—M-1," with the Army designation for model 1" added because the artist, now Chief Warrant Officer Eisner, recalls that Joe was designed "just like a tank." Today both Eisner and Joe are headquartered in the Pentagon.

Joe's mission was to sell preventive maintenance to cut down on necessities for repairs or requisitioning new articles. Ordnance brought Joe into the world to act as a sort of policeman.

Says Eisner: "Joe Dope might save a gun or two from being destroyed by negligence." In the field, officers say his accomplishments are far above those conservative estimates.

Joe spent a year as an exclusive Army ground forces man, but then the air forces requested his services and he took to the air with the same flare for wrong-doing that he had exhibited on the ground.

With appropriate drawings, a typical Dope limerick runs:

"Misled by publicity stuff
Joe Dope feels it's smart to be rough
While driving a jeep—
With a spin and a leap—
Which makes the repairman's job tough!"

Havre de Grace Republican

1868 *The Pioneer Newspaper of Havre de Grace* 1942

HAVRE DE GRACE, SATURDAY MORNING, JULY 4, 1942

FAMOUS CARTOONIST AT O.T.C.

Among the notable men who have come to Harford County's Army camp for training in the Ordnance Department, a recent arrival is **William Eisner, well-known cartoonist and creator of the famous comic strip, "The Spirit."**

Eisner was inducted several months ago at Camp Dix, N. J., before coming to the Aberdeen Proving Ground. He recently became staff artist and writer for "The Flaming Bomb," camp newspaper of the O.T.C. and published by the Havre de Grace Republican.

Among his many contributions to the publication is a new comic strip, "Otis Dogtag," reprinted this week and every week in the Republican by special permission of the Ordnance Training Center Public Relations Department.

Pvt. Eisner's home is in New York City. His famous strip, "The Spirit," is published in the Baltimore Sun.

WAR DEPARTMENT
The Adjutant General's Office
Washington

MEMORANDUM)
No. W45-1-42)

September 7, 1942.

DISTRIBUTION AND DISPLAY OF ORDNANCE MATERIEL PREVENTIVE MAINTENANCE POSTERS

1. A series of posters is being produced designed to improve and emphasize the importance of first and second echelon maintenance, and a quantity of the first poster is being mailed direct to all posts, camps, and stations. The next three posters will be distributed at two-week intervals and thereafter the cadence of distribution of additional posters will be placed on a weekly basis until the series is completed. The posters embody an indirect personal appeal to operating personnel to maintain and care more efficiently for all types of ordnance materiel, and are therefore applicable to the personnel of all organizations.

2. It will be the responsibility of the commanding officers of posts, camps, and stations to arrange for the conspicuous and prominent display of this material in readily accessible locations where it will attract the attention of the greatest number of personnel.

3. It is expected that in some cases the initial shipments will prove insufficient and in some cases excessive. Requests for changes in the quantity of posters, or in the distribution system in general, will be directed to the Office of the Chief of Ordnance, Attention, SPOFM-Preventive Maintenance, Washington, D. C.

(AG 415 (8-28-42) SPOFM-PS)

By order of the Secretary of War:

J. A. ULIO,
Major General,
The Adjutant General.

DISTRIBUTION:
B, C, D.

Eisner in uniform, 1943.

DONT BE A
GABOTEUR
THE ENEMY WANTS TO KNOW WHAT YOU KNOW.
FIGHT THE BATTLE OF WORDS WITH SILENCE.
Remember the enemy fights with words as well as guns
TRAINING DEPARTMENT
O.R.T.C.

Editorial cartoon for *The Flaming Bomb*, January 21, 1943.

EISNER
PLEASE, MR. SOLDIER, DON'T TELL ANYONE ABOUT THAT LAST TROOP SHIPMENT. . . . MY DADDY'S ON IT!"

Editorial cartoon for *The Flaming Bomb*, August 27, 1942.

"I WONDER WHY HARRY MAKKES ME WEAR THIS HORRID DRESS EVERY TIME I VISIT ABERDEEN?"

Editorial cartoon for *The Flaming Bomb*, circa 1942-43.

Bunk Fatigue

GREASE
THANX TO "DENNIS" 4TH ORD. CLASSIF
CPL Will Eisner
"Hello, Classification . . . I'm afraid you didn't quite understand what we ordered."

Bunk Fatigue, panel gag series, *The Flaming Bomb*, circa 1942-43.

BLOW IT OUT Y'R BARRACKS BAG
BY Robin

Column heading, *The Flaming Bomb*, 1943.

PRIVATE DOGTAG . . *"Solid Sleeper"* . . By Pvt. Will Eisner

AHHH.. LET ME SEE.. I'LL HAVE A CHARCOAL BROIL STEAK FOR LUNCH TODAY.. AND HMMM.. I THINK I'LL PUT IN FOR ANOTHER 50 DAY PASS NEXT WEEK..

OH, SERGEANT! I DON'T THINK I'LL GO OUT FOR REVILLE TO DAY
SIR WE'VE DONE EVERYTHING TO HIM.. HE JUST WONT WAKE UP!

Private Dogtag *A New Light* **By Cpl. Will Eisner**

GOSH, HERE I AM THE FIRST ONE IN CAMP TO SEE THE FIRST MINUTE OF THE NEW YEAR.... GUESS THERE'S LOTSA PEOPLE ALL OVER THE WORLD LOOKIN' AT THE SAME SUNRISE AND PRAYIN' FOR US TO MAKE 'EM A HAPPY NEW YEAR!..... SORTA MAKES A GUY FEEL BIG AND KINDA PROUD THAT HE'S GOT SUCH A WHOPPIN IMPORTANT JOB TO DO!

PRIVATE DOGTAG *It's A Frame Up* **By Cpl. Will Eisner**

SORRY DOGTAG, BUT THERE'LL BE NO STRIP THIS WEEK. CPL. EISNER IS QUARANTINED! ONE OF THE MEN IN HIS SQUAD-ROOM CAME DOWN WITH MEASLES!
HAW THAT MEANS I'M OFF TODAY
SGT. LAMAR EDITOR
THINK I'LL GO TO THE SERVICE CLUB HA HA HA HA BOY, IT'S A RIOT... I'LL BET THAT LAME-BRAIN IS STEWIN' LIKE G.I. SOUP RIGHT NOW."
I SAY DOGTAG! DID ANYONE SPRAY RED PAINT ON YOUR FACE?
WHY, NO SERGEANT LAMAR! W-WHY...?
SOME CARTOONISTS HAVE THE SCREWIEST SENSE OF HUMOR
QUARANTIN MEASLES

Private Dogtag *Who's Whose Ol' Man?* **By Cpl. Will Eisner**

Dogtag's Father is in Aberdeen
IN FACT HE'S IN THE SAME COMPANY!
OTIS
THE OL' MAN

I'M SORRY, DOGTAG, YOUR FATHER IS A SOLDIER TOO AND HE MUST TAKE BASIC ALONG WITH EVERYONE ELSE!! NOW, CUT THE GAB!
POOR PAPPY, HE'S GONNA BE 45 NEXT MARCH... GOSH HE AINT NO YOUNGSTER
CN I AT LEAST WALK NEXT TO HIM SARGE? ..P'HAPS I CAN HELP HIM WHEN HE GETS POOPED!
O.K. O.K.

One hour later..
GUESS I WAS A LITTLE ROUGH ON DOGTAG AND HIS OL' MAN!.. POOR OL' DUCK.. I'LL DROP BACK AND GET HIM A LIFT IN THE VULTURE WAGON!

HEY, TOP-KICK WHEN'RE WE GONNA DOUBLE-TIME? WE REALLY WENT ON HIKES BACK IN 1917.. THIS..?? SISSY!

Pvt. Dogtag, a weekly strip Will drew "at night on a foot locker" while stationed at Aberdeen Proving Ground. It was carried in *The Flaming Bomb* and in the local town paper, the Havre de Grace *Republican*. While the New Year's strip is distinctly reminiscent of Milton Caniff's *Terry and the Pirates*, the interplay between Dogtag and his look-alike father is obviously derived from Popeye's discovery of Poopdeck Pappy in Elzie Segar's *Thimble Theatre*. Sgt. (Bob) Lamar, seen in the third strip, was the editor of *The Flaming Bomb* and a close friend of Eisner's. Publication dates for these four strips are, from top to bottom, September 10, 1942; December 31, 1942; January 13, 1943; and February 11, 1943.

WHO HAS THE ONE SPARE PART I NEED TO FIX MY TANK ?!
ORDNANCE DEPT.
CWO Will Eisner
Don't Hoard
SPARE PARTS
U.S. GOVERNMENT PRINTING OFFICE : 1944—O-577520

Joe Dope poster, circa 1944.

PVT. Will Eisner
ORD. TNG. DIV.
Joe Dope is a guy you can't teach-
Here's the way he closes a breech!
When he gets through this chore
On the enemy's shore
They'll spread him all over the beach.
Don't be a dope!
HANDLE EQUIPMENT RIGHT!
ORDNANCE DEPARTMENT, U. S. ARMY

Joe Dope Poster, circa 1944.

?
If the bomb that you aimed like a charm Won't go off and do Japs any harm, Don't declare it's a dud Until you're sure, bud, That you moved that old lever to "ARM."
If lever isn't at "ARM"...
when bomb is dropped it will fall with arming wire still in place

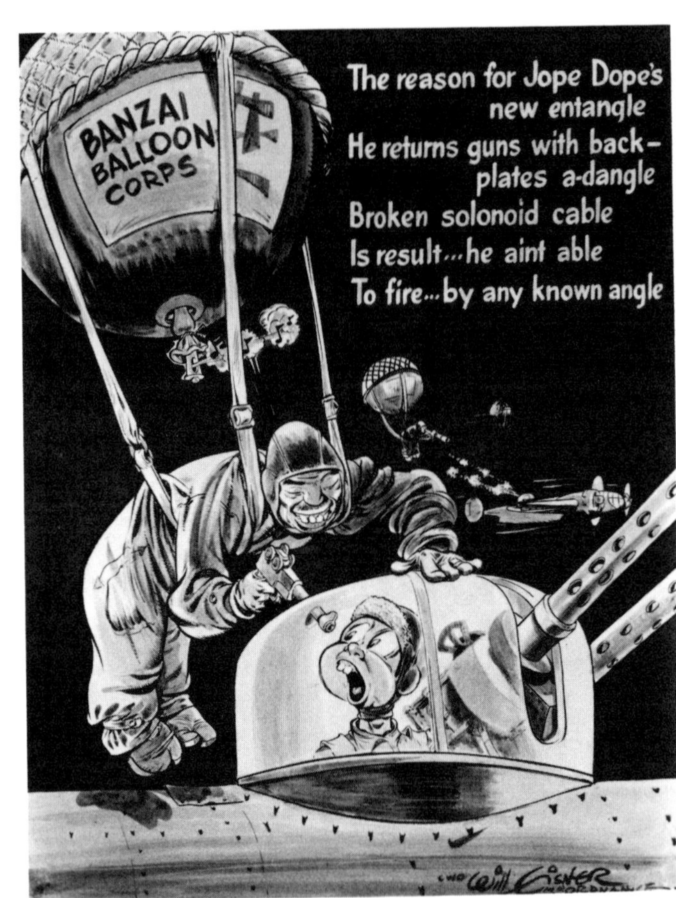
BANZAI BALLOON CORPS
The reason for Jope Dope's new entangle
He returns guns with back-plates a-dangle
Broken solonoid cable
Is result...he aint able
To fire...by any known angle
CWO Will Eisner

DONT WASH VEHICLES IN LAKES, CREEKS OR OCEANS. IT RUINS AND CORRODES DELICATE PARTS

SOAP

CWO Will Eisner ORDNANCE

HANDLE EQUIPMENT RIGHT!

Three of the many *Joe Dope* posters produced between 1942 and 1945.

JOE DOPE.....

JOE DOPE'S FAVORITE MOTTO'S, "PREPARE!"

NO PRECAUTION IS HE KNOWN TO SPARE!
INSURANCE AGAINST EVERYTHING

IN MATTERS OF SEX — YES!

BUT SPEAKING OF WRECKS—GUESS!?

FIRE EXTINGUISHER FAILED....
TNT
AMMO
Will Eisner

.... HAD NO CARE!
PEARLY GATE
RECEPTION CENTER
COMMANDING
ISSUE CLOTHING
WINGS
MP

Don't be a dope!

TAKE CARE OF YOUR EQUIPMENT!

Joe Dope poster using a comic strip approach, circa 1944.

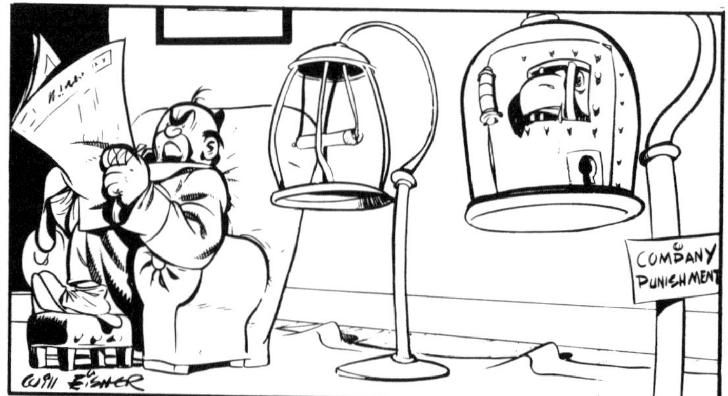

General Poop sample dailies. This was a strip initiated at the syndicate's request, while Will was still in the Army. It was rejected, however, as being "too controvertial."

POODIE, MEET SERGEANT GOLDBRICKER HE WAS MY TOP-KICK WHEN I WAS A BUCK PRIVATE!

BOY... REMEMBER THE DAYS WHEN I USTA GIVE YOU K.P. ...THINGS SURE HAVE CHANGED, EH, GENERAL POOP?

O.K. POOP, LET'S GIT ONA BALL!

Will Eisner

CLICK CLICK!

OFFICERS CLUB DANCE

Will Eisner

ENLIST MEN DANC

These eight *General Poop* strips show the changes Will's signature was undergoing during 1945. By January of 1946, he had settled on the familiar "square" form he still uses.

JOE DOPE IN "ARMAGEDDON"
SPRING 1945...AFTER LONG, TERRIBLE YEARS OF AGONIZING STRUGGLE, THE MIGHTY TIDE OF THE GOOD AND JUST STANDS BEFORE THE CRUMBLING FORTRESS INTO WHICH THE EVIL TYRANTS HAVE RETREATED AND SOUGHT REFUGE FROM THEIR DOOM.... THE FINAL BLOW IS AT HAND!
IN THE ARSENALS OF FREEDOM.... IN THE LANDS OF THE LIBERATED, IN THE VERY BOWELS OF THE EARTH, MEN GIRD THEMSELVES FOR THE CLIMAX THAT IS SWEEPING UPON THEM WITH THE INEXORABLE FORCE OF A SYMPHONIC CRESCENDO!!!!
FACTORIES, MILLS, FORGES.... ALL OPERATING AT PEAK EFFICIENCY— WASTING NOTHING...SPARING NO ONE!

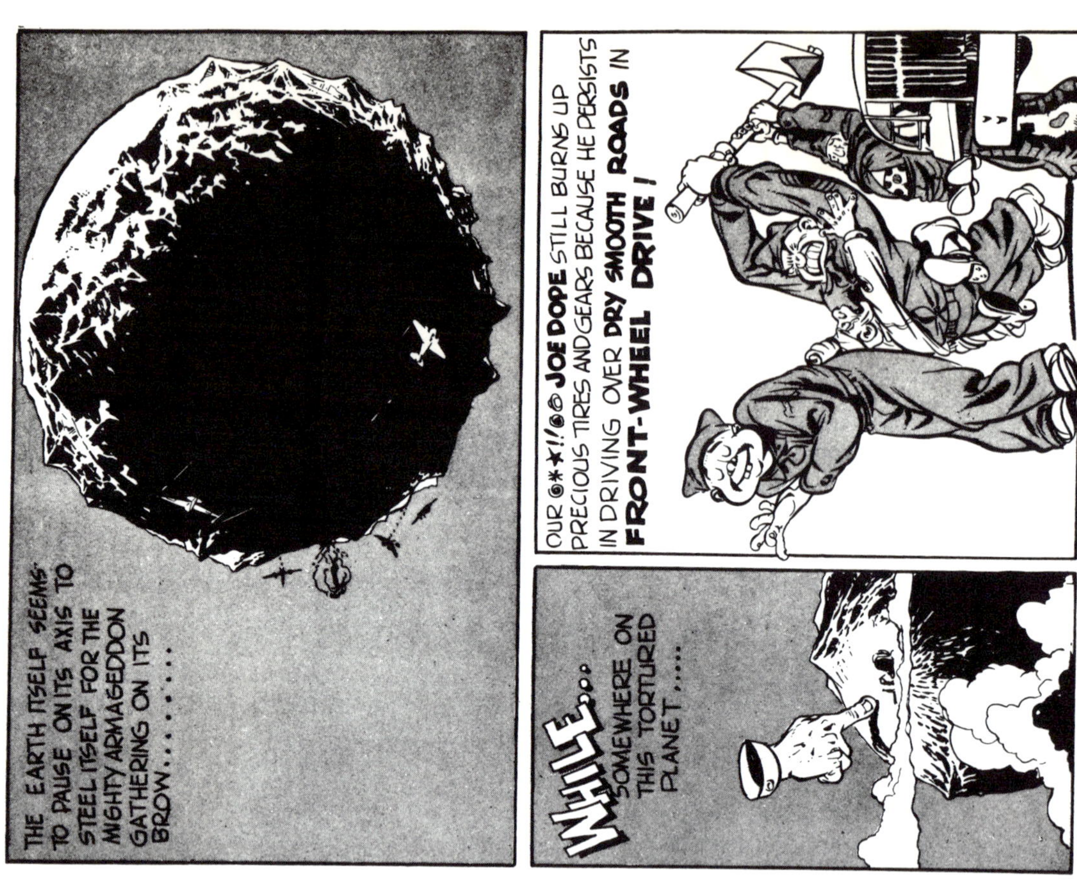
THE EARTH ITSELF SEEMS TO PAUSE ON ITS AXIS TO STEEL ITSELF FOR THE MIGHTY ARMAGEDDON GATHERING ON ITS BROW........
WHILE... SOMEWHERE ON THIS TORTURED PLANET.....
OUR @*✶!!@@ JOE DOPE STILL BURNS UP PRECIOUS TIRES AND GEARS BECAUSE HE PERSISTS IN DRIVING OVER DRY SMOOTH ROADS IN FRONT-WHEEL DRIVE!

Joe Dope strip from *Army Motors*, Vol. 5, No. 12 (March, 1945). Eisner was art director of this magazine, a monthly digest devoted to preventive maintenance. *Army Motors* was the forerunner of the better-known *P*S Magazine*, which is still in publication by the armed services.

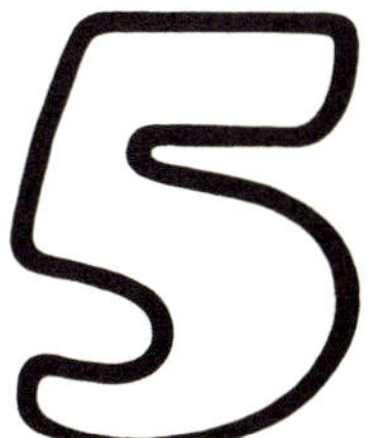

The Spirit and Others: 1945-1952

When Eisner returned to civilian life in 1945, he found *The Spirit* in what could best be called a mess. Poor stories, pedestrian art and the wartime paper shortage had combined to reduce its circulation considerably. Regaining control of the feature, he first set about to rehabilitate it aesthetically and financially. This accomplished in fairly short order, he once more used it as vehicle for his own experimental approach to comic art.

The first post-war *Spirit* by Eisner was published on December 23, 1945. With but a few exceptions, he wrote, pencilled and/or inked a story every week from that date until August 12, 1951, when he once more relinquished it to his assistants.

Several helpers worked with Eisner on the *Spirit* during this time; the practice of keeping assistants is the rule rather than the exception among syndicated cartoonists. Marilyn Mercer, Jules Feiffer and Klaus Nordling contributed occasional plots and scripts. Jack Spranger spent most of 1946 working on either pencils or inks. After he left, Jerry Grandenetti started as a backgrounder, graduated to inking and, toward the end of his tenure, even pencilled some episodes. Jules Feiffer and letterer Abe Kanegson also worked on backgrounds, as did Bob Palmer, but the bulk of the work, from idea to finished page, was Will's alone. It was he who brought to *The Spirit* that unique combination of tragedy, melodrama, humour, intellect, sex, squalor and visual excitement which have made it one of the milestones in the history of sequential art.

A great deal of critical acclaim has attached itself to *The Spirit* over the years. The stories are full of symbolism and shadows; they are drenched in a film noir atmosphere so thick you can cut it with a knife. Just as remarkable are Will's story-telling techniques, his attention to subtle emotional nuances, his bravura lighting effects, his provocative women and his playful self-caricatures. The Spirit is one of those enduring comics which has served as a model for a host of imitations, homages and outright copies. In the words of Jules Feiffer, "Eisner was a cartoonist other cartoonists swiped from," especially when it came to capturing the look of a big city's squalid docks and mean streets.

Eisner at the beach, circa 1946.

THE SPIRIT
BY WILL EISNER
To the north of Central City, on a hill overlooking the bustling metropolis, lies abandoned Wildwood Cemetery. Here, hidden in the tangled weedy growth, is the hideaway of the Spirit. Accepted by the police as a friendly 'outlaw' and feared by the underworld, his true identity is still a mystery. Who is really the man behind the mask? Every so often, someone tries to find out...

Spirit splash page, October 9, 1949 (*The Death of Autumn Mews*). A "symbolic" splash, much like the 1941 example shown on page 41. Once again we see the lone hero projected against the city skyline.

The next 7 pages reprint the complete *Spirit* story of June 12, 1949 (*Hurricane*). As this example demonstrates, the post-war *Spirit* is characterized by a much heavier use of black areas than its pre-war counterpart.

THE SUNDAY SUN
BALTIMORE, MD.

ACTION Mystery ADVENTURE

SUNDAY, JUNE 12, 1949

THE SPIRIT
BY Will Eisner

THE ISLAND OF PUERTO QUE IS ONE OF THOSE COUNTLESS PLEASURE-SPOTS THAT LITTER THE SEA SURROUNDING THE FAMOUS BARBADOS.

BARBADOS, YOU'LL REMEMBER, WAS A FAVORITE SPOT FOR BUCCANEERS OF OLD... TODAY, MODERN BUCCANEERS OF COMMERCE TAKE THEIR PLEASURE HERE IN COMFORTABLE MANSIONS.

IT'S SAFE.. IN FOREIGN TERRITORY... AND PRYING TOURISTS ARE KEPT AWAY BY THE HURRICANES!

NO... I WAS NOT THINKING OF A VACATION...NOR WAS THERE ANY CHANCE I'D SEE A HURRICANE..UNTIL THE DOOR TO DOLAN'S OFFICE SWUNG OPEN...

..AND SHE STEPPED IN..WINDBLOWN AND BEAUTIFUL..WITH AN AGELESSNESS THAT MADE ME THINK OF SORCERY...

SATIN!

AN INSTANT LATER..
SPIRIT.. DARLING.. IT'S BEEN SUCH A LONG TIME...
EASY, EASY... IT'S BEEN A LONG TIME, I'LL ADMIT... BUT BY THE RING ON YOUR LEFT HAND, YOU SHOULDN'T BE THROWING YOUR ARMS AROUND JUST ANY MAN!

I'M MARRIED NOW... TO KURT VAN BRECK.. HE'S AN IMPORTER.. WE MET IN SCOTLAND.. LAST YEAR WE MOVED TO PUERTO QUE IN THE BARBADOS. YOU'D LIKE KURT. HE'S BEEN A WONDERFUL STEP-FATHER TO MY DAUGHTER HILDIE.
SATIN MARRIED.. SIGH... WHEN YOUR FIRST HUSBAND DIED, I THOUGHT... OH, WELL.. I HOPE YOU'RE HAPPY...

I WAS HAPPY, SPIRIT... UNTIL A MONTH AGO, WHEN A MAN ON OUR ISLAND WAS BRUTALLY MURDERED!
HOW DOES THAT AFFECT YOU?

NEXT WEEK, MY HUSBAND KURT WILL BE TRIED FOR THAT MURDER... AND I NEED YOUR HELP... TO PROVE HIM INNOCENT!!

Y-YOU'LL COME, WON'T YOU? I MEAN, EVEN THOUGH HE'S MY HUSBAND..
YOU KNEW I WOULD, SATIN...

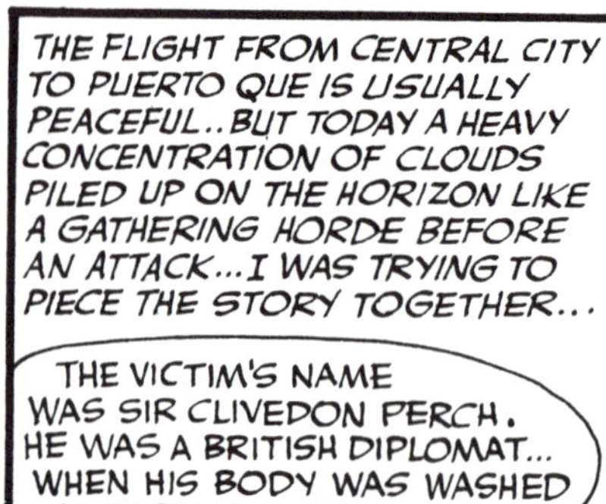
THE FLIGHT FROM CENTRAL CITY TO PUERTO QUE IS USUALLY PEACEFUL.. BUT TODAY A HEAVY CONCENTRATION OF CLOUDS PILED UP ON THE HORIZON LIKE A GATHERING HORDE BEFORE AN ATTACK... I WAS TRYING TO PIECE THE STORY TOGETHER...

THE VICTIM'S NAME WAS SIR CLIVEDON PERCH. HE WAS A BRITISH DIPLOMAT... WHEN HIS BODY WAS WASHED ASHORE, KURT WAS ARRESTED!
...MOTIVE?
THERE'S REALLY NO MOTIVE! THE WHOLE AFFAIR IS RIDICULOUS!
DO YOU REALLY THINK KURT IS INNOCENT, SATIN?

IT DOESN'T MATTER WHAT I THINK! I HAVE A DAUGHTER! HILDIE MUST NOT GROW UP BRANDED A MURDERER'S DAUGHTER! KURT MUST BE PROVED INNOCENT!
FASTEN YOUR SAFETY BELTS! WE'RE COMING IN TO PUERTO QUE!

AS THE PLANE LANDED DEEP IN THE INTERIOR, I COULD SEE THE LIGHTS ON ONE OF THE PLANTATIONS ILLUMINATING THE BLACK JUNGLE THAT COVERED PUERTO QUE.
MUSIC..?
A PARTY. KURT LOVES PARTIES.

UH-OH.. A PLANE HAS JUST LANDED! WE'D BETTER GO BACK TO THE HOUSE, KURT!
2

HMM...YES..THAT'S MY WIFE RETURNING ON THAT PLANE... SEE YOU LATER, SYLVIA.
YES, KURT DARLING.
OH..

BAW!

HILDIE DARLING, I'M BACK! AND I BROUGHT THE SPIRIT WITH ME!

HILDIE!

SATIN, MY SWEET! I HARDLY EXPECTED YOU BACK SO SOON...
KURT DEAR.. THIS IS THE SPIRIT, AN OLD FRIEND OF MINE. HE'S GOING TO INVESTIGATE SIR CLIVEDON'S DEATH AND CLEAR YOU!
?

NICE OF YOU, REALLY, OLD MAN, BUT I WILL SURELY BE ACQUITTED...ER... FLIMSY EVIDENCE! ...WOULDN'T WANT YOU TO..AH.. MUDDLE THINGS UP!
I'LL TRY NOT TO... HANGING IS SO PERMANENT!

HA HA... DELIGHTFUL! WHAT A SENSE OF HUMOR! HA HA HA!!

HE'S YOUR HUSBAND, SWEETHEART! I'LL SEE WHAT I CAN DO!

...I FOLLOWED THE WINDING PATH DOWN TO THE SEA.. A FRESH SOUTHERLY WIND WAS BLOWING IN FROM THE OCEAN...

I STOOD ON THE SPOT WHERE SIR CLIVEDON HAD BEEN FOUND MURDERED... AND AS THE SHARP WIND WHIPPED THE TREES, I HEARD A SOFT SIGHING BEHIND ME, LIKE A CHILD CRYING....
3

WHAT'S THIS ?

THE SURF POUNDING THE SHORE HAD WASHED UP A TATTERED BRIEF CASE WITH A NAME ON IT...
SIR CLIVEDON PERCH !

THE WORLD TURNED BLACK AND GREEN...A HOLLOW ROAR FILLED MY HEAD AND I FELT AS IF I WERE IN THE MIDDLE OF A HURRICANE...
..I DIDN'T KNOW HOW RIGHT I WAS...

HILDIE!
SPIRIT... OH..ARE YOU ALL RIGHT ? I WAS SO WORRIED... THOSE AWFUL MEN!

THEN IT WAS YOU I HEARD CRYING...YOU WERE DOWN HERE WATCHING ALL ALONG! THOSE WERE YOUR STEP-FATHER'S MEN, WEREN'T THEY? ANSWER ME, HILDIE!..FOR YOUR MOTHER'S SAKE...

I WON'T TELL YOU ANYTHING... I DON'T CARE WHAT HE'S DONE ..MOTHER LOVES HIM!
THANKS HILDIE...

I HEADED BACK UP THE WINDING ROAD... THE WIND WAS STRONG AND A GENTLE RAIN BEGAN TO FALL... BUT THIS WAS NOTHING TO THE STORM RAGING WITHIN ME...
KURT WANTED THAT BRIEF CASE PRETTY BADLY... PERHAPS BADLY ENOUGH TO KILL FOR IT!

AS I REACHED THE PORTICO, I HEARD LOUD SHOUTING...
SATIN...YOU FOOL...YOU BUMBLING FOOL... WHY DID YOU BRING HIM?
KURT.. PLEASE.. NOT SO LOUD..

I WAS CERTAIN TO BE ACQUITTED!! ...NOW THAT MASKED MEDDLER WILL RUIN EVERYTHING... GOOD NIGHT!

..BETTER LOOK IN ON KURT...

THE DISPATCH CASE..SO IT WAS KURT'S MEN WHO JUMPED ME...

WELL, WELL... TESTIMONY BY SIR CLIVEDON... HMM... SEEMS THAT KURT VAN BRECK WAS USING HIS IMPORTING FIRM TO SMUGGLE CONTRABAND FROM SOUTH ASIA!

...IF THESE PAPERS GOT AROUND, THEY MIGHT PROVE DAMAGING... MIGHTN'T THEY, KURT?

YES, SPIRIT...AND A MAN MIGHT EVEN MURDER TO GET THESE PAPERS! GIVE THEM BACK TO ME!

KURT, HAVE YOU SEEN HILDIE? I CAN'T FIND HER ANYWHERE! AND STORM WARNINGS ARE BEING POSTED ALL OVER THE ISLAND...A HURRICANE IS RISING!
5

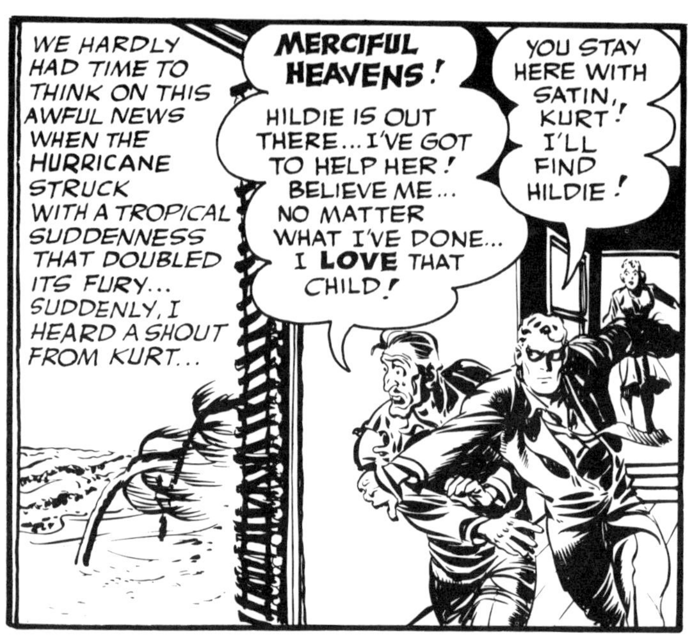
WE HARDLY HAD TIME TO THINK ON THIS AWFUL NEWS WHEN THE HURRICANE STRUCK WITH A TROPICAL SUDDENNESS THAT DOUBLED ITS FURY... SUDDENLY, I HEARD A SHOUT FROM KURT...
MERCIFUL HEAVENS! HILDIE IS OUT THERE... I'VE GOT TO HELP HER! BELIEVE ME... NO MATTER WHAT I'VE DONE... I LOVE THAT CHILD!
YOU STAY HERE WITH SATIN, KURT! I'LL FIND HILDIE!

LET... ME.. GO..

WELL, WHAT DO YA KNOW... THAT SNAKE REALLY LOVES THE KID!

SATIN... HOLD THE FORT... I'M FOLLOWING KURT!
NOT WITHOUT ME, SPIRIT!

WHERE ARE WE GOING?
DOWN TO THE SHORE... THAT'S WHERE I LAST SAW HILDIE...

AN ISLAND BESIEGED BY A MONSTROUS STORM, AND ON IT, THREE MINIATURE FIGURES.... SHOUTING A CHILD'S NAME INTO THE CRAZY WIND THAT FLUNG OUR WORDS BACK AT US.
HILDIE..
HILDIE!
HILDIE!

AND THEN...
SATIN! LOOK OUT!!
C-RA-CK

CRASH

IT'S HOPELESS... IT'S... HOPELESS...
WAIT, SATIN! LOOK... LYING DOWN THERE... IT'S HILDIE!
6

THERE, LYING ON THE REEF, WAS HILDIE, HELPLESS BEFORE THE RAGING SEA...
LOOK, SPIRIT ...KURT IS DOWN THERE!
YES, BY GOLLY... HE'S TRYING TO SAVE HER!

I'LL GRAB HER!

SUDDENLY... THE CLIFF'S EDGE BEGAN TO CRUMBLE...
!
YEOW
??
CRRUNCH

..AND AN INSTANT LATER, KURT WAS SWALLOWED BY THE BOILING SEA..
YAAAAH

SPIRIT!
STAY THERE, SATIN.. HILDIE IS ALL RIGHT...AND KURT...DIED... TO SAVE HER...

IT WAS A LONG TIME BEFORE EITHER OF US SPOKE...BUT AT LONG LAST THE HURRICANE PASSED INTO THE EAST... AND SATIN ASKED ME...
K-KURT.. WAS HE...
KURT DID A GREAT AND NOBLE THING...

NEXT DAY... PUERTO QUE AIRPORT...
SPIRIT... BEFORE YOU GO.. PLEASE... I MUST KNOW... WAS HE GUILTY? DID YOU FIND ANY EVIDENCE?
I..I...HE'S DEAD NOW..IT DOESN'T MATTER ANY MORE... REMEMBER YOUR LATE HUSBAND AS A HERO...
AIRWAYS

I WATCHED SATIN AND HILDIE DISAPPEAR INTO TINY DOTS... AND THE ADVENTURE IN PUERTO QUE WAS BEHIND ME... KURT WAS DEAD... THE EVIDENCE AGAINST HIM COULD DO NO GOOD FOR ANYONE NOW...

SIR CLIVEDON PERCH

I LET THE SCRAPS OF PAPER FLY FROM THE WINDOW AND SCATTER IN THE WIND. THE SKY AHEAD WAS BRIGHT AND THE DAY WAS YOUNG...
REPORT

ACTION
Mystery
ADVENTURE

SUNDAY, JUNE 26, 1949

AS A MATTER OF TRUTH, CRIMEFIGHTERS DEPEND HEAVILY ON SIMPLE TIPS... AND IN THE MATTER OF SNEEVER, THE BOND THIEF, WE HAD THE TIP... AND IT ONLY REMAINED TO PICK HIM UP... A SIMPLE MATTER.. BUT ANYTHING MIGHT HAPPEN..

...WHICH WAS WHY 6:50 P.M. ONE GLOOMY DAY FOUND US AT THE ENTRANCE TO THE CENTRAL BUILDING ON WAFER STREET..

By Will Eisner

From the 65th floor of the Central Building to the street it is but five minutes by elevator. Yet there are times when these few fleeting minutes seem like hours, and the little car a stage wherein mighty dramas begin.... or end...

THE JOINT'S SURROUNDED, SPIRIT... STAIRWAYS AND ALL.. THE ONLY EXIT NOW IS BY ELEVATOR.. WHAT'LL WE DO..?

WAIT

Spirit splash page, June 26, 1949 (*The Elevator*). This page displays one of Will's more imaginative architectural variations on the Spirit logo.

POLICE H.Q.
SPIRIT
BY
WILL EISNER
POLICE H.Q.
CLICK
CLACK
CLICK
CLACK
CLICK
CLACK
CREAK
WHO...?
PUFF
PUFF
CRASH
SPIRIT!
WH..WHAT HAPPENED TO YOU...?
I'M ALL RIGHT... NOW!
... SIT BACK, DOLAN..AND LET ME TELL YOU ABOUT LORELEI...
LORELEI OF ODYSSEY ROAD...

Spirit splash page, September 19, 1948 (*Lorelei Rox*). This splash, with its film noir lighting effects, is a good example of what Jules Feiffer termed "the German Expressionist approach in comics."

Cover, *The Spirit* No. 22 (Quality, August, 1950). Skinny Bones, the subject of this cover, was based on Lauren Bacall.

FOLLOWED BY MILLIONS IN LEADING NEWSPAPERS EVERY WEEK
NOVEMBER No.18
The SPIRIT
BY WILL EISNER
10¢
I.C.D.
11
AND
EBONY
IN
3 SMASH-ACTION
COMPLETE
NOVELETTES
"WHO?"
HAVE YOU EVER WONDERED WHO THE SPIRIT IS BEHIND THE MASK... AND HOW HE CAME TO BE....?
"THE BUCKET O' BLOOD"
"THE RETURN OF Satin"
PLUS
FLATFOOT
BURNS
AND
JONESY

Cover, *The Spirit* No. 18 (Quality, November, 1949).

Cover, *The Spirit* No. 21 (Quality, June, 1950). This cover features P'Gell, the Spirit's most amoral female adversary — and another Bacall-inspired character.

EV'RY LITTLE BUG
Lyric by WILL EISNER
Music by BILL HARR
from the comic strip
GOT A HONEY TO HUG ... BUT ME... SIGH!
The SPIRIT BY Will Eisner
Distributed by the Register - Tribune Syndicate
ROBBINS MUSIC CORPORATION
799 SEVENTH AVENUE · NEW YORK

Cover, *Ev'ry Little Bug* sheet music (Robbins Music Co., 1947). During World War II, Eisner had met Bill Harr when both of them were stationed at the Pentagon producing the Ordnance Department magazine, *Firepower*. The two men remained friends after the war, and when Eisner learned that Harr was a musician, he asked him to compose a melody for a little jingle which had been appearing in *The Spirit* off and on since mid-1946. Although the sheet music was published, the song was never recorded.

Trade Name COMICS

STARRING "SKIP" SUDDEN
TREASUREHUNTER IN 'PIRATE GOLD'
AYE! FINDIN' TREASURE IS ONE THING AND GETTIN' IT BACK WHAR Y' C'N USE IT... IS ANOTHER!
PLUS
GIMMICK The MAGICIAN
FILBY FAMILY
JUNIOR

Cover, *Trade Name Comics* (unpublished, circa early 1947). *Trade Name* was intended to be a syndicated ready-print aimed at the department store market. The art is by Eisner, Jack Spranger and Alex Kotsky, with lettering by Martin DeMuth.

SEARS ROEBUCK

COMICS

PUBLISHED MONTHLY BY SEARS ROEBUCK & CO. FOR ITS PATRONS

RUFF and REDDY
adventures in history
WITH HANNIBAL OVER THE ALPS
GEE WILLIKERS, RUFF... EVERY TIME YOU DREAM SOMETHING HISTORICAL WE END UP IN SOME TROUBLE!
© INDUSTRIAL COMICS

Cover, *Sears Roebuck Comics* (unpublished, circa 1948). This cover was drawn by Eisner, inked by Grandenetti and lettered by Abe Kanegson. The Sears Roebuck Company showed some interest in the idea, but although an eight-page *Ruff and Reddy* story was written and lettered, the project was shelved and the piece was never completed.

Cover, *Pirate Comics* (unpublished, 1948). Jerry Grandenetti inked this drawing over Will's pencils. It was intended to be the third of Eisner's abortive line of self-published newsstand comics. Only the first two titles — *Kewpies* and *Baseball* — ever saw print, and only one issue of each was published.

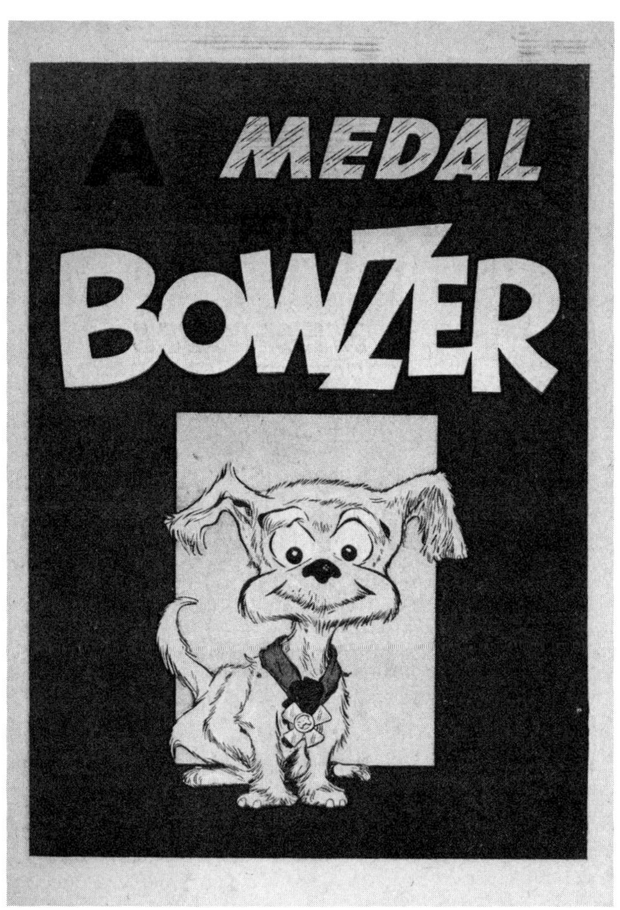

Cover, *A Medal For Bowzer* (late 1940s).

Cover, *The Sad Case of Waiting Room Willie* (late 1940s).

Cover, *Baltimore Colts* souvenir booklet (1950).

In the late 1940s, Eisner founded a commercial art company called American Visuals. The shop produced educational and giveaway comics, primarily for east coast clients. In the early years, Will himself wrote and illustrated the booklets, or at least roughed them out and drew the covers. Above are two comics commissioned by the Baltimore chapter of the American Medical Association. *A Medal For Bowzer* has an Eisner cover and script, with interior art by Klaus Nordling; it deals with the subject of vivisection and urges voters to defeat a local anti-vivisection proposition. *The Sad Case of Waiting Room Willie* has art by Eisner and Nordling and is a tract against socialized medicine. The *Baltimore Colts* program book at left has an Eisner cover, but the interior art — caricatures of the team's members — is by a freelance Baltimore sports cartoonist named Haller.

BOHEMIAN
What A Beer
IN BOTTLES
NATIONAL
BEER
Eisner was a guest on a Baltimore radio show in 1946. *The Spirit* ran in the Baltimore Sun, and Will maintained close ties to the city.

The story of Nubbin the Shoeshine Boy is an exercise in frustration, both for Eisner, who never was able to utilize the character, and for the fan, who is here confronted with an enormous array of incomplete and stillborn concepts. Begun in 1946 as a sample syndicated Sunday page, *Nubbin* was rejected by several syndicates. The character was meant to be, in Eisner's words, "a kind of male Orphan Annie," but he was apparently not "lovable" enough to succeed. Eisner revamped the shoeshine boy and his supporting cast innumerable times over the course of several years before he gave up on the idea at last. There were three entirely different series of *Nubbin* daily strips, a *Nubbin* story scheduled to appear in the never-published *Sears Roebuck Comics,* an abortive *Nubbin* Sunday tabloid ready-print, and two newsstand comic books, also never printed, which featured Nubbin in every story.

On this and the following 18 pages a variety of Nubbin-related material is presented, more or less in chronological order. Much of it was eventually recycled into *The Spirit* in altered form, and a few examples of the latter are shown for the sake of comparison.

Two-page splash panel for *The Half-Dead Mr. Lox,* from *Nubbin Comics* (unpublished, 1948). This tale, in abridged and altered form, was ultimately printed in *The Spirit Section* on February 19, 1950.

NUBBIN
THE SHOESHINE BOY
AND THE STRANGE, GHASTLY AFFAIR OF THE
HALF DEAD
MR. LOX

First week, *Nubbin* daily series No. 1, *Riverbend* (unpublished, 1946). Below and on the next page are the five remaining dailies for the first week of a *Nubbin* series by Will Eisner and Alex Kotzky. Episode no. 2 (Tuesday) is missing. This plot was recycled (with entirely new art) in the *Spirit Section* of June 18, 1950. Judging from that version, which starred Willum Waif, the man we see here as Nubbin's father will turn out to be an impostor and will die in short order, presumably during the second, third or fourth weeks of this sequence, which are missing.

RIVERBEND... POPULATION 10,000
CHILDREN TAKE YOUR SEATS
HYA JOEY
SOMEONE PUT GUM ON MY SEAT
RIVERBEND ELEMENTARY SCHOOL
SCHOOL OPENS TODAY

WELL, BOYS AND GIRLS I KNOW THAT YOU ARE ALL GLAD TO BE BACK AT SCHOOL AGAIN!
PHOOY!

I WANT YOU ALL TO MEET A NEW CLASSMATE.... NUBBIN BUTTS
AW, WE ALL KNOW HIM MISS FEAVER.. HE'S ONLY THE SHOE SHINE BOY OF RIVERBEND.

YOU NEEDN'T JEER, MORTON! SHINING SHOES IS AN HONEST LIVLIHOOD.
OH, YEAH? THEN WHAT'S THE COP OUTSIDE WANT NUBBIN FOR?

JUMPIN JITNEYS. I SURE HATE TO LEAVE SCHOOL ON THE FIRST DAY.. WHAT'S PA IN FOR NOW ?
SAME OLD CHARGE, NUBBIN. ...SWINDLING

SIGH POOR PA, I WUNNER HOW I'M EVER GONNA TAKE CARE OF HIM NOW THAT I'M GOIN' T'SCHOOL FULL TIME!

Y'R HONOR .. I PROTEST THIS INDIGNITY... I SOLD THAT WATCH TO THIS MAN IN GOOD FAITH ...AN HONEST TRANSACTION !

IT WOULD HAVE BEEN HONEST, BUTTS... IF YOU HAD INCLUDED THE WORKS.....

NUBBIN, THE LAST TIME I RELEASED YOUR FATHER IN YOUR CUSTODY YOU PROMISED ME HE WOULD STAY OUT OF TROUBLE.
HULLO JUDGE FAIRLEE

NOW, HE'S BACK FOR SWINDLING MR. QUINCE OUT OF $30.
...AND UNLESS I GET MY MONEY BACK SIGMUND BUTTS Y'R GOIN' T'JAIL!

YOUR HONOR, ALL I NEED IS A FEW DAYS...I'M ABOUT TO EMBARK UPON A PROJECT THAT WILL NET ME A COOL $50,000.
YAWWN .. YOU GOT ANY MONEY NOW

...ER AH AHEM... ... AH .... THAT IS... ...NO!
I HAVE IT JUDGE

YOU MEAN... YOU HAVE $30 TO PAY BACK MR. QUINCE?
YES Y'R HONOR HERE IT IS!

VERY WELL, CASE DISMISSED.....BUT THIS TIME I ORDER YOU, SIGMUND BUTTS, TO LEAVE TOWN...I'M SORRY SON... BUT THAT'S THE DECISION OF THIS COURT
RAP! RAP!

WELL NUBBIN, LAD, Y'SURE SAVED Y'R PA THAT TIME...WHERE'D Y'EVER GET THAT $30.?
SAVED IT OUTA MY SHOE SHINE BISNISS..10 CENTS A DAY FER A YEAR

WHY YOU LITTLE SNIPE...AND ALL THE TIME Y'PRETENDED TO GIVE ME ALL OF YOUR EARNINGS!

AW, GEE PA...'JUS' WHEN I WUS STARTIN' SCHOOL ....YOU HADDA CHEAT MR. QUINCE AN' GOT US ORDERED OUTA RIVERBEND!

AHH SHUT-UP...WHAT DO YOU WANT WITH SCHOOL ... POOF!

WHY, I NEVER SPENT MORE THAN TWO WEEKS IN SCHOOL AND LOOK AT ME NOW...A SELF-MADE MAN....

ER...AHEM..I SAY NUBBIN, LAD COULD YOU LEND ME THE PRICE OF A CIGAR?

LOOK OUT LADY! LOOK OUT FER THEM FELLERS!
?

WELL, HOWDEEDOO MISS FEAVER STILL SOCIAL WORKIN' IN SLUMGULLY NOW, WE TOL' YIZ ONCE BEFORE TO KEEP OUTA HERE!
LET GO YOU APE!

HEY! LEGGO OF HER YOU GUYS!
SHINE 5¢

GIVE ME THOSE PACKAGES YOU THUGS...THEY'RE FOR MRS. PAUPER, THE WIDOW!
DON'T WORRY LADY I'LL RESCUE YOU!
!

WHOP!
?

WE AINT GOT NOTHIN POISENUL 'GAINS YOU MISS FEAVER.... IT'S JUST THAT OUR BOSS DON'T WANT YOU HANDIN' OUT CHARITY TO THE POOR IN SLUMGULLY! DON'T COME BACK AGAIN, SEE!
JUST TRY TO STOP ME YOU GREAT BIG BRAVE, HEEL!

JUST A MOMENT... WHO IS THIS BOSS OF YOURS?

WELL, EX-PFC. MERVIN MEATAXE! I HAVEN'T SEEN YOU SINCE I COURT MARSHALLED YOU IN ITALY... WHO IS THIS BOSS YOU BEAT UP WOMEN FOR?
LIEUT. MEDIC... IN CIVVIES!

BOY! I USTA DREAM OF A BREAK LIKE THIS, MEDIC...WHEN YOU AN'ME WOULD MEET AS CIVILIANS AGAIN... NO RANK BETWEEN US! I'D DREAM I WAS GONNA SLUG YIZ RIGHT INNA SNOOT... AND, NOW, THAT'S WHAT I'M GONNA DO!

GOLLY HE'S SMILING... GUESS HIS DREAMS ARE GETTIN' BETTER ALLA TIME, LIKE THE SONG SAYS!

TOO BAD I HAD TO KNOCK YOU OUT, MEATAXE ... YOU SURE TELEGRAPHED THAT PUNCH! —NOW, BEAT IT!
YAA.. YOU WAIT MEDIC.. WE AINT IN THE ARMY ANY MORE.. I GOT A LOT TO SETTLE WITCHA, NOW!

HA.. I'LL SAY HE HAS... I WAS CAPTAIN OF HIS COMPANY —MEDICAL CORPS— BACK IN ITALY... CAUGHT HIM SMUGGLING DOPE TO BLACK MARKETEERS... HE WOULD HAVE BEEN SHOT BUT FOR THE BOYS IN THE COMPANY WHO BEGGED THAT HE MERELY BE DISCHARGED... NOW HE'S A CIVILIAN HOOKED UP IN SOME RACKET.... SAME OLD MEATAXE!

WONDER WHO HE'S WORKING FOR MISS ER.... ?
ER I KNOW! MR ... ER ??

WELL, IF Y'LL TELL ME Y'R NAMES I'LL INTERDUCE YA BOTH!

Fifth week, *Nubbin* daily series No. 1, *Riverbend* (unpublished, 1946). The only episodes remaining from this week are numbered 3 through 6 (Wednesday through Saturday). As before, the work is by Eisner and Kotzky. The pipe-smoking Lieut. Medic seems to be a forerunner of John Law, minus the eye-patch incurred by a war wound.

OL' GAFFER'S JUNK YARD SANCTUARY AND HOME FOR THE ORPHAN NUBBIN
HELP!
SOME-ONE'S IN MY JUNK PILE!

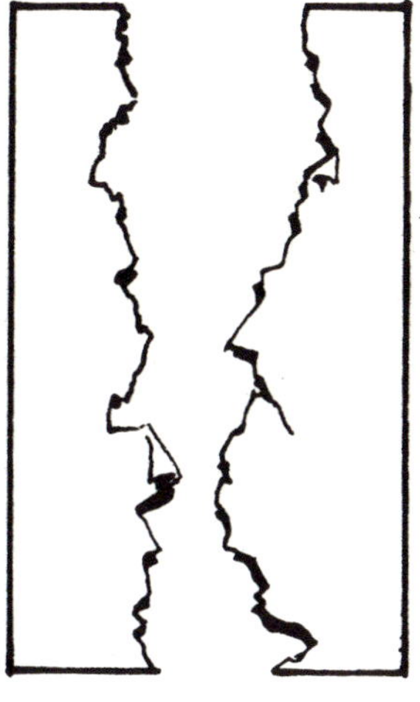

THEY CAN'T DO THIS TO DR. NUCLEAR P. FISSION! I'LL SUE!
SNORT ... IT'LL DO YE LITTLE GOOD! WE HAVEN'T GOT A CENT TWIXT US!

AHA! POOR, EH?? GOOD! YOU ARE JUST THE MAN I'VE BEEN SEEKING ... HERE'S $25! SEE ME IN MY OFFICE TOMORROW WITHOUT FAIL! YOU ARE ON THE THRESHOLD OF IMMORTALITY.... MY CARD....

DR. FISSION, I HOPE THIS MAN IS THE RIGHT TYPE...
AN OLD JUNKMAN AND A LITTLE SHOESHINE BOY? HMM... HARDLY PEOPLE OF ANY CONSEQUENCE!
PRECISELY WHY I HAVE CHOSEN THEM... AFTER ALL, WHAT HAVE THEY GOT TO LOSE?

MAYBE WE SHOULDN'TA SPENT ALL OF THE 25 DOLLARS DR. FISSION GAVE US ON A HAT!
NUBBIN', WE ARE ON THE THRESHOLD OF IMMORTALITY AND I AIM TO CROSS IT DRESSED FOR THE OCCASION!
DR. N. P. FISSION

HOWDY, DR. FISSION! WE'RE HERE... I'M GAFFER, PRIVATE, U.S. ARMY, RETIRED! THIS IS NUBBIN!
AH... RIGHT ON TIME! NOTICE, HE IS PUNCTUAL!

First week, *Nubbin* daily series No. 2, *Moon Trip* (unpublished, 1947). The original artwork for the first week of this *Moon Trip* series by Eisner and Kotzky was cut apart and re-used for the *Tab Section* (page 87). In the process, some panels were lost. The top tier on this page contains three panels from the first two dailies. The second tier is the uncut art for the third strip (Wednesday). On this tier are the two remaining panels from the Thursday strip. Below are the last three panels from the Friday episode.

NOW TO WORK! WE ARE A GROUP OF HARD-HEADED REAL ESTATE MEN! WE WANT YOU TO GET TO THE MOON BEFORE ANY OTHER EARTHLING AND BUY UP ALL THE PROPERTY YOU CAN... WE'LL MAKE A FORTUNE!
CAN'T YOU SEE IT NOW... 'LUNAR LOW COST HOUSING DEVELOPMENT"?

HA, HA, HA! ONE WOULD THINK WE WERE GONNA JUMP OFF THE EARTH!

PRECISELY WHAT WE HAVE IN MIND!

OH... WELL THAT'S DIFFERENT! WHEN DO I START?
TOMORROW!

HAVE YOU GOT A ROCKET SHIP THAT'LL REACH THE MOON ?
CERTAINLY!! WE'VE BUILT THIS JET PROPELLED TWO SEATER WITH RADIO AT AN ESTIMATED COST OF $15,526.04!

MIGHTY CHEAP... Y'CAN SEE, NUBBIN, THAT WE'RE BEIN' BACKED BY HARD-HEADED BUSINESS-MEN!
BUT, GAFFER... SUPPOSE WE DON'T GET BACK GULP ALIVE!
U.S.A. SURPLUS PROPERTY

AHA! WE'VE PROVIDED FOR THAT!
YES! WE'VE INSURED YOUR LIVES FOR $25,000! IF YOU SHOULD FAIL TO RETURN WE MAKE A PROFIT OF $9,473.96!
Y'SEE, NUBBIN, M'LAD! THAT IS SOUND BUSINESS THINKING!
?

GAFFER AND NUBBIN HAVE BEEN TALKED INTO PILOTING DR. FISSION'S PLANE TO THE MOON... ....AFTER BEING INSURED FOR $25,000 OF COURSE!
WILL EISNER

GAFFER, MY GOOD MAN, WE WANT YOU TO KNOW THAT WE, YOUR SPONSORS, WILL REMAIN BEHIND HERE TO SUPPORT YOUR EXPEDITION!
AHEM... THIS REMINDS ME O' THE TIME I SET OUT TO KETCH PANCHO VILLA... AYE, AS I CROST THE BORDER....
HSST! PULL THE STARTER!

...THERE WUZ THAT SAME LOOK IN FOLKS' EYES AS I RODE OUTTA TOWN...

CALL THE INSURANCE COMPANY AND FIND OUT HOW SOON AFTER DEATH WE, HIS BENIFICIARIES, CAN COLLECT THE INSURANCE!

GOLLY, I REALLY DINT THINK THIS OL' SURPLUS PLANE COULD FLY... BUT WE'RE UP!
AYE, NUBBIN M'LAD! AH!! A RADIO... I'LL REPORT!
WILL EISNER
CRASH
?

LUNAR EXPEDITION... GAFFER, IN CHARGE, REEPORTIN'... AIMIN' SHIP AT MOON... PUTS ME IN MIND O' THE TIME I ENLISTED WIF CUSTER'S RIDERS ...WAS NO OLDER'N NUBBIN HERE... WELL, SIR, I SAID T'MAW, I SEZ BLA, BLA, BLA, BLA B...

YEP! IT'S COMFORTIN' T'KNOW WE HAS A GROUP O' LOYAL FRIENDS SUPPORTIN' US BACK ON EARTH!
WE JUST NABBED 'EM, Y'R HONOR! THEY WUZ REPORTED BY THE ACME INSURANCE COMPANY!
NUCLEAR P. FISSION, EH?? HMPF! THIS IS THE FOURTH TIME HE'S BEEN BROUGHT UP ON SWINDLE CHARGES! LAST TIME HE INSURED A MAN WHO WAS ABOUT TO TUNNEL A SUBWAY TO CHINA! THIS TIME I'M GOING TO THROW THE BOOK AT YOU!!

First and second weeks, *Nubbin* daily series No. 2, *Moon Trip* (unpublished, 1947). The top tier is the last (Saturday) strip for the first week. The first two strips of the second week follow. The third daily from that week (Wednesday) is missing completely, and at right is the last panel of the Thursday episode, the only one which remains.

AT THAT MOMENT... NOT FAR AWAY....
STOP EVERYTHING!! I'VE GOT AN IDEA THAT'LL REACH THE MOON!
DISCOUNT AND HUCKSTER
RADIO ADVERTISING PRODUCTIONS
STUDIO B

WHAT *IS* YOUR IDEA, MR. HUCKSTER?
EVERYTHING IS GEARED FOR SPLIT SECOND TIMING! I'LL EXPLAIN AS WE PROCEED! *LISTEN!* OUR SHOW IS COMING ON THE AIR NOW!
WILL EISNER

THIS IS THE MOONGLOW PERFUME HOUR ··· THE PERFUME OF THE MOON
SMELL THAT MOOOONGLOW!! PHEW! AHHHHHH PHEW!! NO OTHER PERFUME CAN MAKE THIS STATEMENT! ···AND NOW A SPECIAL ANNOUNCEMENT FROM OUR SPONSOR ···

LAST WEEK, OVER THIS PROGRAM WE SENT A MESSAGE TO THE GODDESS OF THE MOON VIA A NEW U.S. ARMY SHORT WAVE DESIGNED FOR STRATOSPHERIC COMMUNICATION!
GET IT, P.D.?
ER, *NO,* MR. HUCKSTER!

AT THAT MOMENT·····
WHEE··· SAYS 7,500 MILES PER HOUR ··· WE'LL MAKE THE MOON IN NO TIME AT THAT RATE!
THAT'S THE *ALTIMETER* GAFFER··NOT THE SPEEDO-METER.!!
GO
GO
WILL EISNER

CAME FROM
PLANET!
HUCKSTER
LETS GET OUT OF HERE THE TOWNS PEOPLE WILL ARRIVE ANYMOMENT!! THIS HAS GOTTA LOOK LEGIT

WE'VE LANDED! NUBBIN, M'LAD··· DON'T Y'FEEL LIKE COLUMBUS?
IF HE HAD A BUMP ON HEAD, I DO!
JUGVILLE GO SLOW
US 10

SOME ONE IS HIDING BACK THERE I'LL LOOK.....!

?

WILL EISNER

GOLLY, MISS STAR! IF IT WASN'T FOR YOU WE'D NEVER ESCAPED THOSE CROOKS··· GOSH, WILL YA EVER BE ABLE TO GO BACK TO JUGSVILLE AGAIN?
WELL, HARDLY···I DON'T THINK ANYONE WILL EVER BE ABLE TO CONVINCE THEM THAT POOR GAFFER *REALLY* BELIEVED HE WAS ON ANOTHER PLANET!

POOR GAFFER IS STILL UNCONSCIOUS!
HOLD ON, NUBBIN! THE TRAIN IS GOING AROUND A CURVE···

WILL EISNER
EEK!

AHA! WE'RE BACK ON EARTH AGAIN···

Second through sixth weeks, *Nubbin* daily series No. 2, *Moon Trip* (unpublished, 1947). The top two tiers are the Friday and Saturday strips of the second week. The next tier is unnumbered and probably ran during the third or fourth week. The bottom tier is the first (Monday) episode of the sixth week.

The third *Nubbin* daily series, *The Thing*, was scripted and lettered for ten weeks' worth of story, but only a few panels were pencilled, and even fewer inked. The plot centered on a mysterious locked box given to Nubbin by Mr. Shadrock, whose life he had saved. Con man Eazy J. Munny and his girlfriend, Melba Tost, want the contents of the box. When finally opened, the container appears to be empty, except for the words, "The Thing." written on the bottom. Nubbin is befriended by the invisible "Thing," a genie who helps him shine shoes. Meanwhile, a Russian (?) submarine enters the harbour and mysterious people kidnap Nubbin, Shadrack, Munny, Tost and others...

JUMPIN' JITNEYS! I C'N HARDLY WAIT TO SEE WHAT'S IN THE BOX! WHAT DOES FABULOUS WEALTH MEAN, MR. KEYS?
IT MEANS WEALTH BEYOND TELLING... A WEALTH THAT IS USUALLY DESCRIBED BY FABLES LIKE KING MIDAS! ...UGH! I'LL HAVE IT OPEN IN A JIFFY, NUBBIN....

Inked panel, Eighth week, fourth day of *Nubbin* daily series no. 3, *The Thing* (unpublished, 1947).

GAFFER
WELL EF IT AINT MOLD PAL ABE LINCOLN!
DID YOU KNOW HIM GAFFER?
AND NUBBIN BY Will Eisner
YA WELL READ ON LINCOLN?
NO
THEN I CAN SPEAK FREELY!
IN ME YOUTH... DURIN' THE INJUN TROUBLE ON M'WAY THRU ILLINOIS I MET UP WITH HIM A-TRYIN' T'FELL A TREE
SEZ I, "ABE," ALL Y'NEED IS THE GAFFER METHOD"." SEZ HE, "PROVE IT!" SEZ I, "I'LL GIVE YE A HANDICAP AFORE I EVEN START!"
NEVER SEED SECH A SURPRIZED MAN!
?
OH, GAFFER, THAT'S A WHOPPER! WHY LINCOLN WAS A CHAMPION RAIL SPLITTER!!
OH YEAH? THEN HOW COME HE QUIT TH' WOODS FER A CHAIR JOB DOWN T'WASHINGTON D.C.

Gaffer Sunday page, featuring Nubbin (unpublished, 1946). When this proposed Sunday strip was rejected by the syndicates, Eisner planned to use it in *Sears Roebuck Comics*, a project which in turn was abandoned before publication.

"tab"
THE
COMIC
WEEKLY

COPYRIGHT, 1947, SUNDAY SUPPLEMENTS CORPORATION

HUMOR
ADVENTURE
MYSTERY

DIST. BY McCLURE NEWSPAPER SYNDICATE

Nubbin

BY ALEK KOTT

OL' GAFFER'S JUNK YARD SANCTUARY AND HOME FOR THE ORPHAN NUBBIN
HELP!
SOME-ONE'S IN MY JUNK PILE!

THEY CAN'T DO THIS TO DR. NUCLEAR P. FISSION! I'LL SUE!
SNORT ... IT'LL DO YE LITTLE GOOD! WE HAVEN'T GOT A CENT TWIXT US!

AHA! POOR, EH?? GOOD! YOU ARE JUST THE MAN I'VE BEEN SEEKING ... HERE'S $25! SEE ME IN MY OFFICE TOMORROW WITHOUT FAIL! YOU ARE ON THE THRESHOLD OF IMMORTALITY.... MY CARD....

NEXT DAY
HOWDY, DR. FISSION! WE'RE HERE... I'M GAFFER, PRIVATE, U.S. ARMY, RETIRED! THIS IS NUBBIN!
AH ... RIGHT ON TIME! NOTICE, HE IS PUNCTUAL!

NOW TO WORK! WE ARE A GROUP OF HARD-HEADED REAL ESTATE MEN! WE WANT YOU TO GET TO THE MOON BEFORE ANY OTHER EARTHLING AND BUY UP ALL THE PROPERTY YOU CAN... WE'LL MAKE A FORTUNE!
CAN'T YOU SEE IT NOW ... 'LUNAR LOW COST HOUSING DEVELOPMENT"?

HA, HA, HA! ONE WOULD THINK WE WERE GONNA JUMP OFF THE EARTH!

PRECISELY WHAT WE HAVE IN MIND!

HAVE YOU GOT A ROCKET SHIP THAT'LL REACH THE MOON?
CERTAINLY!! WE'VE BUILT THIS JET PROPELLED TWO SEATER WITH RADIO AT AN ESTIMATED COST OF $15,526.04!

MIGHTY CHEAP... Y'CAN SEE, NUBBIN, THAT WE'RE BEIN' BACKED BY HARD-HEADED BUSINESS-MEN!
BUT, GAFFER... SUPPOSE WE DON'T GET BACK GULP ALIVE!
U.S.A. SURPLUS PROPERTY

AHA! WE'VE PROVIDED FOR THAT!
YES! WE'VE INSURED YOUR LIVES FOR $25,000! IF YOU SHOULD FAIL TO RETURN WE MAKE A PROFIT OF $9,473.96!
Y'SEE, NUBBIN, M'LAD! THAT IS SOUND BUSINESS THINKING!
?

AT THAT MOMENT... NOT FAR AWAY....
STOP EVERYTHING!! I'VE GOT AN IDEA THAT'LL REACH THE MOON!
DISCOUNT AND HUCKSTER
RADIO ADVERTISING PRODUCTIONS
STUDIO B

YOU KNOW THEY'LL NEVER REACH THE MOON.. WE KNOW THEY WON'T... BUT DO NUBBIN AND GAFFER KNOW IT?

CONTINUED NEXT WEEK

Tab Section (unpublished, 1947). The second (*Moon Trip*) series of *Nubbin* dailies was cut apart and reworked for use as a Sunday supplement called the *Tab Section*. This was credited to "Alek Kott" (Alex Kotzky) because if the Tab Section had proved successful, Kotzky would have taken over the feature completely. The McClure syndicate handled Tab, but although Eisner remembers at least one being published, no printed copies have ever been found.

Designs for another version of *Nubbin*, this time with dark hair. The other characters, developed at the request of the syndicates, are reminiscent of Ham Fisher's *Joe Palooka* and Al Capp's *Li'l Abner*.

GOSH, SPRING SURE IS PRETTY OUT HERE…LOOKIT HOW THE WHOLE CITY IS LIT UP!
SIGH!

SOMEDAY SOON, THAT CITY WILL BE **YOURS!** EVERY ONE OF THOSE TINY LIGHTS REPRESENTS A FAMILY WHO WILL SOON KNOW ABOUT **FIREBALL BAMBINO!**
BUT I DON'T REALLY WANT TO BE FAMOUS!

I SORTA THOUGHT WE…THAT IS…WE…WELL, A LITTLE GIRL LIKE YOU, CAN'T RUN A BIG JUNK-YARD ALL ALONE!

Nubbin daily series No. 4, *Fireball Bambino* (unpublished, 1947). The only artwork from this sequence still in existence are these three panels from an unnumbered daily. The fourth panel is missing, but Nubbin appears ready to rush in and break up baseball pitcher Bambino's clinch with his girlfriend.

Fireball Bambino was reworked in late 1947 and became Rube Rookie, star of *Baseball Comics*. This was Eisner's attempt at publishing comic books for newsstand sales, and it failed after only one issue, due to poor distribution. Jules Feiffer wrote the script and Tex Blaisdell assisted Eisner on the art. The back-up feature, recounting a famous historical baseball game, was the work of Feiffer and *Spirit* assistant Jerry Grandenetti. Eisner published a second comic at the same time, entitled *Kewpies*. This one contained no Eisner artwork at all. It was written by Jules Feiffer and illustrated by ex-Disney studio artist Lee J. Ames and *Spirit* assistant Andre Le Blanc. It also carried Feiffer's first published strip, *Clifford*. Although *Kewpies* — based on the famous Rose O'Neill characters — was a failure, *Clifford* went on to become the permanent page 8 back-up feature in *The Spirit*.

RUBE ROOKY

NEW YORK!
ROOKY, EH?? SORRY, POP… CAN'T USE HIM!
BUT….
ER 'M NOT LOOKING FOR NEW TALENT THIS YEAR…. HRUMPH!! SORRY….
NOPE… SORRY, POP!
MISS LASH? POP FLYE WAS HERE PEDDLING HIS PITCHER…. **NATURALLY** I TURNED HIM DOWN AS YOU…ER… SUGGESTED…NOW ABOUT THAT LOAN YOU PROMISED US….
?? WHAT A BRUSHOFF! BUT **WHY??**
WELL! **POP FLYE!** I HAVEN'T SEEN YOU SINCE THE '34 CARD-TIGER SERIES! HEAR YOU GOT A **NEW PITCHER!**
Y'HEARD RIGHT! ARKY! BUT IT 'PEARS **HIM** AN' **ME** IS BOTH OUT IN THE COLD!
BOOTS SHORE
GENTS! I WANT Y'SHOULD MEET THE ONE AND ONLY **POP FLYE!**
WHO??
POP FLYE!
OH!
YOU GUYS MUST REMEMBER "BAFFLER" FLYE…TH' FOG BALL ARTIST O' TH' 1908 VIOLETS! HE'S GOT A GREAT NEW PITCHER….
SO I HOID! SO I HOID! TOO BAD YOU'LL **NEVER** SELL 'IM!
THE WAY LANA LASH IS FIXIN' THE SQUEEZE, YOU'LL HAFTA **BUY** A TEAM TO GET YOUR BOY A TRYOUT! HA! HA! IT'S SAID TH' FLATSWAMP BADGERS ARE UP FOR SALE!
LANA LASH!! I SHOULDA KNOWED!!!
THE BADGERS… HUMPH! **THEM?** WHY THAT DUNGEON TEAM FINISHED EIGHTY-FI' GAMES OUT LAST YEAR!!
SNAP
TUT! TUT! JES' BAD MANAGE-MENT! NOW IF **YOU** WORKED THEM RIGHT, POP… Y'MIGHT…Y'**MIGHT** BUILD A CLUB! CHUCKLE
GOLLY….YEAH…. IT'S WORTH THE CHANCE!! O.K…. **WHO OWNS THAT TEAM??**
ME!!
I HAD TO HOCK THE TROPHY OL' TY COBB GIMME TO MAKE THE PRICE, BUT IT WAS WORTH IT…..NOW **RUBE** CAN **PITCH** WITH A **TEAM!!**
HAW! WAIT'LL HE SEES WHAT HE BOUGHT!!

Baseball Comics (Eisner, Spring, 1948).

Unfinished cover, *Nubbin Comics* (unpublished, 1948). Like Nubbin himself, the proposed back-up feature, *Melba, Girl Detective*, was borrowed from the defunct *Tab* section. The character of Nubbin's friend, policeman John Law, apparently proved more attractive to Eisner than did that of the shoeshine boy, because he was soon promoted from proposed back-up feature to co-star, and eventually became the lead feature of the comic.

NUBBIN
SO YOU WANT TO HEAR MY TRUE LIFE STORY, EH, NUBBIN?
BET IT'S EXCITIN', BEIN' A REAL DETECTIVE AN' ALL!

Partially inked splash page for a *John Law* back-up story in *Nubbin Comics* (unpublished, circa 1947). This was the splash for an abandoned story called *Sand Blue*, a few lettered pages of which still exist. *Sand Blue* was subsequently rewritten as *Meet John Law*, and Sand Blue herself was renamed Sand Saref. After some alterations in both script and art, *Sand Saref* was eventually published as a two-part *Spirit* story on January 8 and 15, 1950.

Pencilled cover rough for *John Law Comics* (unpublished, circa 1948). When Nubbin was demoted to the back-up slot, John Law's confrontation with Sand Blue/Sand Saref became the projected cover story.

THE COACH'S BENCH

A MAN-TO-MAN BULL SESSION ON REAL AROUND-THE-BLOCK QUESTIONS THAT AFFECT US ALL...

Conducted BY JOHN LAW -

THIS IS YOUR DEPARTMENT

Artwork for a text feature page in the proposed *John Law* comic (unpublished, 1948).

The closest Nubbin and company ever got to print was in *John Law Comics*. This was meant to be the fourth of Eisner's self-published comics, but with the immediate failure of *Baseball* and *Kewpies,* it and *Pirate Comics* never went farther than the dummy stage. Three complete stories were produced for *John Law*, two of them starring Nubbin. The lead feature was the rewritten Sand Blue story, now eleven pages long and co-starring Sand Saref. The back-ups were *The Half-Dead Mr. Lox* and *Ratt Gutt* .

After *John Law* was abandoned, Eisner kept the material on the shelf for two years. In 1950, all three *John Law* stories, plus two pieces from the never-printed second issues of *Kewpies* and *Baseball*, were adapted for use in *The Spirit* and published at last. Luckily, stats were made before the original art was subjected to the alteration process. In those days the value of comic book artwork was nil, and Eisner thought nothing of cutting up pages, spreading white-out over word balloons and covering extensive portions of the artwork with rubber-cemented paste-overs. In this way Nubbin was redrawn as Willum Waif or Sammy as occasion demanded, John Law became The Spirit, and Police Commissioner Bunyan was transformed into Police Commissioner Dolan, as shown below.

YES..YES... WHAT? WHEN... YEAH... NO THANKS... I'LL LET YOU KNOW IF I NEED ANY MORE
F'GOSH SAKES, LAW..SPILL IT! ..WHAT'S IT ALL ABOUT?

A panel from page 6 of *Meet John Law*, the lead feature for *John Law* No. 1 (unpublished, 1948).

YES. YES... WHAT? WHEN... YEAH... NO THANKS... I'LL LET YOU KNOW IF I NEED ANY MORE
F'GOSH SAKES, SPIRIT..SPILL IT! ..WHAT'S IT ALL ABOUT?

The same panel, altered by pasteovers, appears on page 2 of *The Second and Final Installment of 'Sand Saref,'* published in *The Spirit* on January 15, 1950.

Splash page for *Sunday* Comics, starring John Law and Nubbin (unpublished, 1948). This was meant to be a ready-print like *The Spirit Section*, but was never syndicated. Evidently Nubbin and Law's encounter with the Half-Dead Mr. Lox was to be the interior story for this first issue. This cover was cut apart and re-used several times, as shown on the following pages.

Cover, *John Law Comics* (unpublished, 1948). This was the cover for the dummy *John Law* comic designed for newsstand distribution. Sand Saref has replaced Nubbin as the co-star of the book.

The SPIRIT
SECTION

ACTION
Mystery
ADVENTURE

SUNDAY, MARCH 12, 1950

the SPIRIT
BY Will Eisner
$\sqrt{\frac{3}{\text{THIEVES}} + \frac{1}{\text{TREASURE}} + \frac{1}{\text{GREED}}} =$
IN THE ALGEBRA OF CRIME THERE IS
NO MORE DEADLY EQUATION THAN THIS

Spirit splash page, March 12, 1950 (*The Jewel of Gizeh*). The *John Law* cover was finally printed as the first page of a *Spirit Section* in which Sand Saref — now a regular member of the supporting cast — made an appearance. Unfortunately, the scene depicted here has absolutely nothing to do with the interior story. It was taken from the original *Meet John Law/Sand Saref* episode, of course, but *The Jewel of Gizeh* is a Middle Eastern adventure story. Ironically, when Warren Publishing Co. began reprinting *The Spirit* in 1974, Basil Gogos was commissioned to paint the cover for issue no. 1, and he based it on this splash page. Later, a fifth version of the same illustration (by Eisner) was printed as a poster. Thus the "definitive" illustration of Denny Colt is in reality John Law with a mask!

JOHN
LAW
WHEREVER MEN LIVE, BE THEY NOMADS OR CITY DWELLERS, THERE THEY MUST HAVE A LAW AND A MAN TO ENFORCE IT WHO IS STRONG, DECENT, AND BELIEVES IN THE RULES HE DEFENDS.
SUCH A MAN IS DETECTIVE JOHN LAW OF THE CROSSROADS CITY POLICE.
THE TIDE IS OUT, AND ON THE GLISTENING GREASY FLATS YOU WILL FIND THE HARVEST OF CRIME... WHERE, AT THE START OF A TRAIL... YOU CAN
MEET JOHN LAW...

Splash page for *Meet John Law*, the 1948 story co-starring Sand Saref which was scheduled to run in the unpublished *John Law Comics*.

THE SPIRIT

ACTION
Mystery
ADVENTURE

SUNDAY, JANUARY 15, 1950

IT WAS THREE A.M. WHEN THE RELIEF FOUND PATROLMAN FISK LYING BADLY WOUNDED ON THE FROSTY MUD FLATS IN THE BAY... AND ALL THAT WAS LEFT BY THE EBBED TIDE WAS A SINGLE CLUE... A SCRAP OF PAPER CLEARLY LABELED... "SAND SAREF"... USUALLY IT WOULD BE A ROUTINE MATTER... BUT SAND SAREF WAS MY CHILDHOOD SWEETHEART... AND NO MATTER HOW I TRY TO AVOID IT... I KNOW THAT ARRESTING HER WILL BE THE HARDEST TASK OF MY CAREER.

THE SECOND AND FINAL INSTALLMENT OF

"SAND SAREF"

BY

WILL EISNER

Splash page for *The Second and Final Installment of 'Sand Saref.'* When the eleven-page *Meet John Law* was remade into a fourteen-page *Spirit* story, three new pages of art were added at the beginning. The original splash (at left) was cut apart and reworked, becoming the splash page of the second seven-page installment, published January 15, 1950.

A JOHN LAW TRUE TO LIFE ADVENTURE
THIS IS THE STORY OF ROGER GUTT... THE KIND OF OPERATOR YOU READ ABOUT IN THE HEADLINES...
ROGER (RATT) GUTT FREED
ONCE AGAIN THE WELL KNOWN HOODLUM IS FREED ON BAIL
MAYBE THERE'S A GUY LIKE HIM WHO HANGS AROUND YOUR NEIGHBORHOOD... YOU KNOW THE KIND... BIG SHOT..CONVERTIBLE WITH WHITE WALL TIRES..LOTS OF MONEY..FLASHY GIRLS...CLOT

RATT GUTT
...A LOT OF KIDS ENVY HIM ...YOU KNOW... SORT OF ADMIRE THE WAY HE PUSHES FOLKS AROUND...
WELL... HERE'S A CLOSE-UP PICTURE OF JUST SUCH A GUY...

Two-page splash for *Ratt Gutt* from *John Law Comics* (unpublished, 1948).

The third story in the dummy *John Law* comic book of 1948 was *Ratt Gutt*. It co-starred Nubbin and John Law and was a typical morality tale. Originally eight pages in length, it featured an unusual double-page splash, shown above. When it was adapted for use in *The Spirit*, it was trimmed down to the standard seven page length by giving it the new one-page splash shown at right. The published story contains numerous pasteovers by Eisner, transforming Nubbin into Willum Waif and John Law into Denny Colt.

ROGER (RATT) TRAPP FREED
ONCE AGAIN THE WELL KNOWN HOODLUM IS FREED ON BAIL
THIS IS THE STORY OF ROGER TRAPP...THE KIND OF OPERATOR YOU READ ABOUT IN THE HEADLINES...
MAYBE THERE'S A GUY LIKE HIM WHO HANGS AROUND YOUR NEIGHBORHOOD... YOU KNOW THE KIND...BIG SHOT..CONVERTIBLE WITH WHITE WALL TIRES..LOTS OF MONEY..FLASHY GIRLS...
...TO A LOT OF THE KIDS WHO LOAF ABOUT AFTER SCHOOL, HE'S A SORT OF HERO... A WHEEL... A GUY WHO CAN DEFY THE LAW AND NEVER GET CAUGHT...
...AND THAT WAS HOW HE APPEARED TO TOMMY ROCCS AND WILLUM WAIF UP UNTIL ONE AFTERNOON...
THE SPIRIT
BY
Will Eisner

Splash page for *Ratt Trap* from *The Spirit* (January 29, 1950).

6 Commercial Art: 1951-1979

Despite the failure of the *Nubbin* projects and the swift demise of *Baseball* and *Kewpies* comics, Eisner's educational comic book company, American Visuals, prospered and soon began to occupy most of Will's time. The output of the American Visuals staff was divided into two kinds of comics. The first, dealing with what Will calls "attitude conditioning," provided propaganda for subjects as diverse as job, vacation and fire safety; political campaigns and dental hygiene. The second type of comic, which teaches what Eisner refers to as "product procedures," gave simple technical drawings a lift by adding humorous characters who acted out the care or repair of the products in question.

Based on ideas he developed during his *Army Motors* days, Will's best educational comics combine instructions with propaganda. In effect, they "sell" the reader on proper maintenance while giving step-by-step instructions on how to do it. Of these, the long-running Army magazine, *P*S*, which Eisner's company produced for twenty years, was the most successful. *P*S* employed a staff of eight artists and writers, including three technical illustrators. Some of the people who worked on it over the years include Dan Zolnerowich (former *Sheena* artist), Klaus Nordling, Murphy Anderson, Mike Ploog and Chuck Kramer. Eisner roughed out most of the illos, drew the covers and the eight-page comic insert starring Joe Dope, and oversaw the liaison with a 24 man staff supplied by the Army to determine what the contents of each issue would be. The first few years of *P*S* are distinguished by some fine work by Will, particularly his parodies of *Dragnet* (called *Hairnet*) and his use of film noir effects to add surreal "drama" to a plug for careful engine lubrication. The messages — check your spark gap, never over-inflate tires, give your truck a spring tune-up — are simple, but the method of presentation is extravagant and engaging. Although Eisner terminated his connection with *P*S* in 1972, it continues to be published to this day, under the direction of Murphy Anderson.

As Eisner told John Benson in an interview, it was the success of commercial ventures such as *P*S* and *Hoods Up* (a comic produced for the Fram Oil Filter company) which spelled the eventual demise of *The Spirit*. "...*The Spirit* began to become very burdensome, because I was doing hundreds of other things...I'd just gotten married...and the whole Sunday newspaper market was beginning to soften. So I had to make a decision. I could have continued *The Spirit*, I suppose, and I thought about it very seriously, but I finally decided I would close the show while it was ahead."

Eisner the commercial artist, circa 1960.

Eisner left the field of adventure comics completely from 1952 to 1978. Most of his work during this period consisted of educational material of one sort or another: *Job Scene*, a series of comics for the Department of Labor; *America's Space Vehicles*, a hardbound textbook containing no comics at all; *Grammarfun*, an illustrated supplement for elementary English classes; and a host of other obscure and specialized items. During these years Will also produced a small body of entertainment comics, but none of them contained extended fictional narratives. Most were gag cartoons or illustrations for humour books. Examples range from the record sleeves he drew for RCA to the several *Gleeful Guides* to modern life he wrote and illustrated. Along the way Will also turned out a few commercial art projects for advertising campaigns such as New York Telephone's *Rip Roscoe* series extolling the virtues of touch-tone phones. Not as stunningly original as his fictional work, these drawings merely serve the purpose for which they were intended, never transcending the limited boundaries of their form.

Record sleeves drawn by Eisner in 1957 and 1958, using gag ideas supplied by Bernard Miller. Eisner and Miller had met during the war and remained friends after being discharged. Miller worked for RCA Victor, a company which, until it signed Elvis Presley away from Sun Records, was known for its staid and conventional performers. The rock'n'roll revolution, with its attendent payola scandals, provided Miller with much amusing material for record sleeves designed solely for promotional distribution to disc jockeys. Of the picture sleeves shown on these two pages, only one — The Singing Dogs' novelty tune, *Hot Dog Rock'n Roll* — was used on a general release pressing.

ER...AHEM...NOW, WHICH ONE OF YOU GIRLS SANG INTO THAT OPEN MIKE HERE LAST NIGHT?
©1957 Will Eisner

TRANSLATION: 'WE'VE GOT A HOT RECORD THAT'S OUT OF YOUR WORLD'

The XYZ LABEL Co
RECORD LABELS WITH A HEART
SINCE 1903
I DONT KNOW HOW THE RECORD BUSINESS IS DOIN'...BUT I TELL YA, RIGHT NOW THE LABEL BUSINESS IS TERRIFIC!!
©1957 Will Eisner

KEEP YOUR*!✶© SHOES SHINED... IT'S GUYS LIKE YOU WHO GIVE ROCK 'N ROLL A BAD NAME
©1957 Will Eisner

DEPT. ARCHAEOLOG
AMERICAN CULTURE
HORSE
1995 JULY
PROF. J.J. KINKLY AMERICAN CULTURE
...AND HE WAS APPARENTLY ONE OF THEIR GODS NAMED "OLVIS" OR "EELVIS" AND THEY USED TO SIT AROUND AND LISTEN TO HIS MESSAGES ON LITTLE ROUND DISCS CALLED VECTIRS OR VICTORS
© Will Eisner 1958

ARE YOU KIDDIN'? ...WHY, THERE ARE DOZENS OF WEEZAPHONE FANS IN THIS TOWN...

...don't take it... remember what the boss said about "Payola"...
P. 1713 Litho in U.S.A.

THATS RIGHT... WAY BACK IN THE WOODS WE FOUND HER...WHY, WE DIDN'T EVEN KNOW SHE WAS A GIRL!!

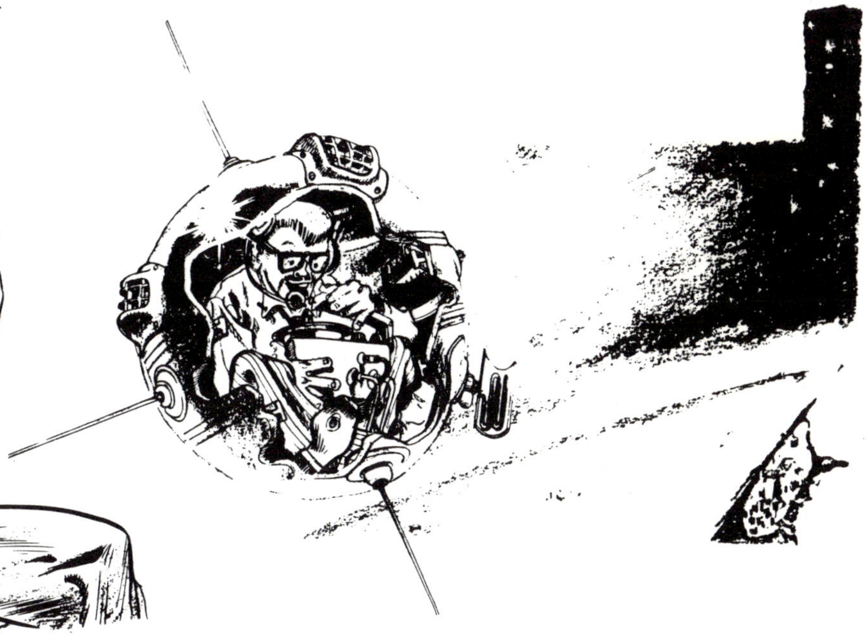

RCA
SURE IT'S AN EMERGENCY... THEY'VE GOT A HOT RECORD!

Litho in U.S.A.

RCA VICTOR
47-6432
DON CHARLES presents
THE SINGING DOGS
directed by
CARL WEISMANN
"Hot Dog Rock 'N Roll"
"Hot Dog BOOGIE"

This book is dedicated to the GHOSTS of folks who had DEADLY IDEAS

CHIEF GHOST

...IF YOU WANT TO JOIN US GHOSTS, HANG ON TO THESE DEADLY IDEAS!

Splash page, *Deadly Ideas*, 1952.

The advent of the Korean War gave Eisner an opportunity to recommission Joe Dope, Connie Rodd, Sgt. Half-mast and Pvt. Fogsnoff (all *Army Motors* alumni). After an initial testing period in which the comic book approach was evaluated against standard training manuals, *P*S, The Preventive Maintenance Monthly,* became a regular government publication. For a time Eisner drew a weekly *Joe Dope* strip for Army camp newspapers, but this was discontinued shortly. Connie Rodd, the beautiful and efficient mechanic who co-starred with Joe Dope in the *P*S* comic section and hosted her own advice column, did double duty as Convertible Connie for the Fram Oil Filter comic book, *Hoods Up.* In this series, the usually knowledgeable Connie appears in the guise of a typical customer at Earl Philter's service station, while Earl and his sidekick, Argyle McSludge, present oil filter sales tips and installation advice. Another Eisner comic from this period, *Deadly Ideas,* was distributed by General Motors to its employees as part of a job safety program.

Cover, *Hoods Up* No. 3, May, 1953.

P*S
THE PREVENTIVE MAINTENANCE
SEPTEMBER - OCTOBER 1952 NUMBER 9
HOW TO MEASURE HIGH ANGLE CANT
see page 390

Cover, *P*S* No. 9, September-October, 1952.

P*S
THE PREVENTIVE MAINTENANCE MONTHLY
NUMBER 11
Brother, you're not just kidding

Cover, *P*S* No. 11, January-February, 1953.

JOE DOPE
IN THE SPRING A TUNE-UP
Now, the sun....
coasting closer
from the far edge of our orbit
Breathes its warm sweet breath on the land
Here a bird trills
There a saplet glistens
Now the winter hard soil
yields to man
Over at mess hall 3
a bud pouts
An insect hums
And the mess sgt.
his heart aburst
with gladness
sings...
GIT THIM
COVERS ON THIM
GARBAGE CANS...Y'WANT WE SHOULD HAVE FLIES AGAIN THIS SUMMER!!
MOTOR POOL
Yes, Spring is here!

Splash page, *Joe Dope*, from *P*S* No. 18, 1954 series.

AH, CONNIE, TIS SPRING AGAIN, THE BIRD IS ON THE WING AGAIN... ...TELL ME, BABE, WHAT DOES IT MAKE YOU THINK OF?
I BLUSH TO SAY, JOEY!
COME ON BABY, YOU CAN TELL ME
I AM THINKING YOUR VEHICLE SHOULD HAVE A SRING TUNE-UP.
1. ANTI-FREEZE
DRAIN IT AND STORE IT IN FIFTY GALLON DRUMS YOU GET FROM QM!
2. CLEAN & FLUSH COOLING SYSTEM
BLOW OUT RADIATORS ...OOOPS
I AM!
POP
GOT A PIN?
NO... I'M BUSY CHECKING THE THERMOSTAT.

Story panels, *Joe Dope*, from *P*S* No. 18, 1954 Series.

JOE DOPE

Reportin' For Duty

By WILL EISNER

MOTOR POOL BY GRAVY
?
HA HA HAW HAW
HA HA HA HA
1

OKAY, KNOCK IT OFF...WOT'S THE GAY LAFFTER ABOUT..??
HEY SERGEANT SHORTPANTS... DIDJA SEE THIS GOOF-OFF CHARACTER THEY GOT IN P.S. MAGAZINE? BOY! WOT A SHNERK!!
IT'S A NEW HOT G.I. MAINTENANCE MAGAZINE..LIKE THE OLD "ARMY MOTORS"..REMEMBER ??
LOADING A TRUCK IS A ART!

DO I REMEMBER! WHY, I SPENT 4 YEARS IN THAT STUPID @#*-- JOE DOPE'S OUTFIT! FOR 4 LONG YEARS I WATCHED HIM DESTROY MORE VALUABLE EQUIPMENT THAN TWO NAZI PANZER DIVISIONS. IN MY TIME I SEEN JOE LOUSE UP REQUISITION PROCEDURES... RUN VEHICLES WITHOUT OIL... CHEW UP TIRES BY UNDER-INFLATING...YAHHH PTOOY!
HOW I HATE EVEN HIS MEMORY!!
DOPE SHEET
WE HAVE THE WORLDS
PRODUCED UNDER SPECIAL LICENSE TO U.S. DEPT. DEFENSE COPR. 1951 WILL EISNER PRODUCTIONS

H'YA
SERGEANT SH... PANTS, HERE'S THE NEW CASUAL REPLACEMENT... WANNA ASSIGN HIM A...?
PLEASE, SERGEANT, DON'T DO IT! WE'RE STILL UNDERMANNED!
!!
WILL EISNER

JOE DOPE

Together Again

By WILL EISNER

BOY OH BOY..JUST THINK... JOE DOPE AND SERGEANT SHORTPANTS TOGETHER AGAIN...EVEN IF IT'S KOREA...GOSH, TO THINK I GET CALLED BACK UP AND ZZT!..I'M RIGHT BACK IN YOUR OUTFIT AGAIN!
+!!!

LOOKS LIKE LOTS OF COMMIE ACTION UP IN THE HILLS... GLAD YOU GIMME THIS DELIVERY... I WANT A CHANCE TO SHOW YOU I'M ON-THE-BALL!!
2
WILL EISNER
PRODUCED UNDER SPECIAL LICENSE TO U.S. DEPT. DEFENSE COPR. 1951 WILL EISNER PRODUCTIONS

YES SIREE, SARGE. Y'KNOW, I'M NO DIFFERENT FROM ANYBODY ELSE..I LEARN. I MAY HAVE BEEN THE BIG GOOF-OFF OF WORLD WAR II... BUT I'VE CHANGED. I...

THE TRUCK... IT STOPPED ON ME....

THIS VEHICLE HAS A CRUISING RANGE OF 200 MILES. ALL OVER KOREA WE HAVE GAS-UP STATIONS EVERY 50 MILES ...A-N-D Y-O-U RUN OUTTA GAS!!

JOE DOPE

No Skins Out Of My Wallet

By WILL EISNER

AHH, MY GOOD FRIEND PRIVATE JOE DOPE. WHAT MANNER OF GRIM TIDINGS COULD CAUSE SUCH DISTEMPER?
... GOT A LETTER FROM HOME IN THE LAST MAIL CALL!

SO ??...ACCEPT PLEASE MOST SINCERE CONDOLENCE. PERHAPS BELOVED FIANCEE HAS JILTED YOU... OR FAVORITE DOG HAS GONE TO ANCESTORS?
WORSE! ME OLD MAN HAS CUT MY ALLOWANCE. NOW I GOTTA LIVE ON MY G.I. PAY AND I'VE BEEN RED-LINED T'BOOT.
PRODUCED UNDER SPECIAL LICENSE TO U.S. DEPT. DEFENSE COPR. 1951 WILL EISNER PRODUCTIONS

BUT... WHY DOES PARENT DO THIS??
AAAH... HE SAYS THAT IN ORDER T'PAY F'R MILITARY ARMAMENT THEY INCREASED TAXES AT HOME...SO THE OLD MAN'S TAKE-HOME PAY IS LESS.. SO, I GET CUT..
UH OH!

SUPP ROOM
WHAT AGAIN?? THIS IS THE THIRD YOU TORE UP THIS WEEK... THIS STUFF COST DOUBLE WHAT IT DID IN '45!
AHHH. THIS ACCOUNTS FOR PARENTAL PENURY!

JOE DOPE

They Do It All The Time

By WILL EISNER

AHH, GOOD MORNING MOST DISTINGUISHED PRIVATE JOE DOPE.. THE HONORABLE GUARDIAN OF YON ORDERLY ROOM ASSIGNS ME TO AID YOU IN THE DELIVERY OF PRECIOUS PARTS TO A FORWARD AREA...
I AM HONORED, MY CONSCRIPTED KOREAN COMRADE... SOON AS I FINISH WELDING.

YOU WILL NOTICE HOW, BY PLACING THE BEADS IN THE FOLLOWING MANNER I CAN WELD THESE SPRINGS IN A JIFFY...
OH PRIVATE DOPE YOU ARE INDEED CLEVER.

AND ON THE ROAD, LATER...
?
CLANG! PLANG PINK
PRODUCED UNDER SPECIAL LICENSE TO U.S. DEPT. DEFENSE COPR. 1951 WILL EISNER PRODUCTIONS

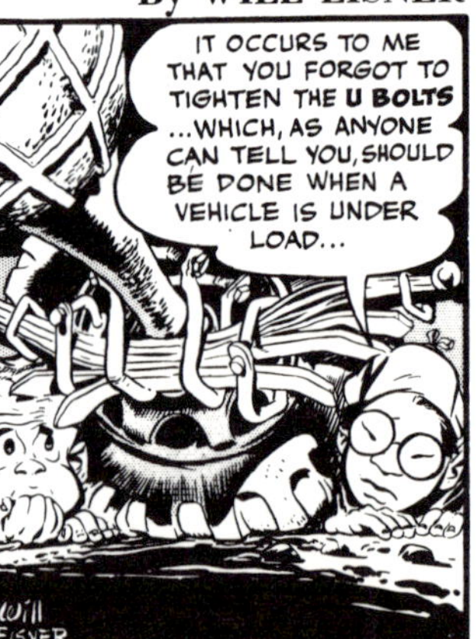

IT OCCURS TO ME THAT YOU FORGOT TO TIGHTEN THE U BOLTS ...WHICH, AS ANYONE CAN TELL YOU, SHOULD BE DONE WHEN A VEHICLE IS UNDER LOAD...
WILL EISNER

Joe Dope strips No. 1-4, 1951.

JOE DOPE — Yeah . . . T/O Sure Is Loaded — By WILL EISNER

HYA CONNIE!
...HEY JOE, C'MON LET'S LOAD THEM OIL DRUMS AWREDDY!
?
CONNIE RODD'S BASE SHOP SCHOOL
PRODUCED UNDER SPECIAL LICENSE TO U.S. DEPT. DEFENSE COPR. 1951 WILL EISNER PRODUCTIONS

WHY JOSEPH DOPE I HEARD YOU WERE BACK IN THE SERVICE, BUT I NEVER DREAMED THEY'D ASSIGN YOU OUT HERE...YOU WERE SUCH A GOOF-OFF!
WHY... C-O-N-N-I-E RODD...YOU DO ME A SUPREME INJUSTICE!
WILL EISNER

THAT MAY HAVE BEEN TRUE BACK IN '42... BUT NOW I AM A OLDER-WISER-SOLDIER...WHY I'M A ASSET TO ANY T/O
OKAY.. OKAY... SAVE THE SNOW JOB!
CRASH

WHO LEARNED YOU TO LOAD A TRUCK....
I THINK OUR T/O HAS JUST BECOME TOO CROWDED!
5.

JOE DOPE — . . . And Nobódy Cares For Me — By WILL EISNER

OH I AIN'T GOT NOBODY
OKAY OKAY SHADAP AWREDDY WILL YUH ???

WHAT'S WITH YOU AND JOE DOPE, CORPORAL?
AHHHH.... SERGEANT, THAT MEAT-HEAD USED A OLD SCRAP STEEL BOLT AS A SHEAR PIN IN MY WINCH DRUM!
PRODUCED UNDER SPECIAL LICENSE TO U.S. DEPT. DEFENSE COPR. 1951 WILL EISNER PRODUCTIONS

WHY, CORPORAL FARFNUFFEL THAT (AS ANYBODY KNOWS) IS DANGER-OUS... WHY MAN ALIVE, THAT PIN MIGHT BE MADE OF STEEL SO HARD IT WOULD HOLD BEYOND THE CABLE'S SNAPPING POINT... AND SOME DAY...UNDER LOAD.. (WHEN YOU LEAST EXPECT IT) POP THE CABLE WILL SNAP... AND SNICK
6.

OH SERGEANT SHORTPANTS, YOU ARE SO RIGHT.... I AIN'T GOT NOBODY
WILL EISNER

JOE DOPE — What's A Coupl'a 'C' Notes To Us Taxpayers — By WILL EISNER

HYA, JOE DOPE...C'N I BORRY YER WALKIE TALKIE?
SURE, WHAT'S HAPPENED TO YUH?

THE BOLTS ON THE SPROCKETS OF ME TANK WAS NEVER TIGHTENED... AND SOB THEY SHEARED OFF FROM THE VIBRATION ...TANKS USELESS... NOW WE'RE IN A FORWARD AREA SO I GOTTA CALL BACK TO THE AIRFIELD AN' HAVE 'EM DESTROY IT... SIGH
TSK...TSK... MAN, THAT TANK COSTS US $200,000 ...WHAT LAZY FOOL COULD HAVE BEEN SO WASTE-FUL WITH OUR TAX MONEY?
7.

PRODUCED UNDER SPECIAL LICENSE TO U.S. DEPT. DEFENSE COPR. 1951 WILL EISNER PRODUCTIONS
YOU!!
WILL EISNER

JOE DOPE — I Got A Date With A Dream — By WILL EISNER

WHY, MARLENE SHAKUPP! THE GREAT ENEMY SPY WHAT ARE YOU DOING ON MY BUNK?

I AM HERE TO PAY YOU FOR THE GAS TANK CAPS YOU HAVE BEEN SWIPING. INDEED, THIS BIT OF FIVE-FINGER REQUISITIONING FOULED UP THE FUEL PUMPS AND CARBURE-TORS OF 100 VEHICLES IN THIS SECTOR ALONE...NAME YOUR REWARD ANYTHING.......ANYTHING!

HERE'S THE GAS TANK CAPS I BEEN ER... SWIPIN'...I'LL EXPLAIN LATER... RIGHT NOW I GOTTA GET RIGHT BACK TO SLEEP!
WILL EISNER
8.
PRODUCED UNDER SPECIAL LICENSE TO U.S. DEPT. DEFENSE COPR. 1951 WILL EISNER PRODUCTIONS

Joe Dope strips No. 5-8, 1951.

JOE DOPE — Higher Mathematics — By WILL EISNER

WE'VE GOT A COUPLE OF VEHICLES DEADLINED AND OUR OUTFIT'S ON ITS WAY TO THE PORT...I WAS SENT DOWN TO SEE IF YOU HAVE ANY EXTRA PARTS!
COMPANY SUPPLY ROOM
NO!!
ON DUTY JOE DOPE

PLEASE.... JOE...PLEASE... WE NEED 2 GENERATORS! HOW MANY DO YOU HAVE?
A EVEN DOZEN!
PRODUCED UNDER SPECIAL LICENSE TO U. S. DEPT. DEFENSE
COPR. 1951 WILL EISNER PRODUCTIONS

THAT'S GREAT...WITH YOUR 12...YOU ONLY NEED HALF THAT.... SO HOW ABOUT TRADING ME 2 FOR THESE TWO OLD ONES?
NOPE!

WHY? WHY??
CAUSE IF I LEND YOU 2, THEN I WON'T HAVE AN' EVEN DOZEN!

JOE DOPE — They'll Do It At The Port — By WILL EISNER

HEY, JOE... WE'RE SHIPPIN' OUT TOMORROW. GIT ON THE BALL AND READY-UP Y'R JEEP!
NOT FORGETING OF COURSE, TO PROPERLY CRATE FOR SAFETY AROUND THE WINDSHIELD!
FRAGIL
CARE
SACK TIME

AAAH...THEY'LL DO IT AT THE PORT!

...AT THE PORT
AAAH...THEY'RE SUPPOSED TO CRATE IT AT THE PORT... IT'SA 2ND ECHELON JOB!
CRASH

...ABOARD SHIP
AAAH...THEY SHOULDA BOXED IT AT THE PORT!
BANG

DESTINATION...
YOUR MOTOR POOL REPLACEMENTS, SIR!!
...LOOKA' THE WAY THEY HANDLED MY NEW JEEP...I'LL WRITE TO ME SENATOR I'LL PROTEST!
PRODUCED UNDER SPECIAL LICENSE TO U. S. DEPT. DEFENSE
COPR. 1951 WILL EISNER PRODUCTIONS

JOE DOPE — Bearing Up Under Pressure — By WILL EISNER

WHEEEEEEEEEEEEEE
AIR-RAID ??
?
?
PRODUCED UNDER SPECIAL LICENSE TO U. S. DEPT. DEFENSE
COPR. 1951 WILL EISNER PRODUCTIONS

WHEEEEEEEE
GRRRR...
LOOK MA,...I'M A SIREEN
WHAT A COMEDIAN!

GRRRR LAST WEEK I CAUGHTCHA TAPPIN' OFF BEARINGS WITH A HAMMER INSTEAD OF USIN' A SOFT PIPE AN' NOW THIS!
AW SARGE,.... WHUTCHA SO SORE ABOUT? I WUS JUST DRYIN' THEM BEARINS WITH A AIR HOSE ...AND I DISCOVER IT MAKES A NOISE LIKE A SIREEN.

WHAT BEARINGS! WHAT WAS ONCE NICE ROUND STEEL BALLS, Y'JUST WORE DOWN T'SHAPLESS PEBBLES!

JOE DOPE — Borrowin' From Peter To Pay Paul — By WILL EISNER

WELL WE GOT A PROBLEM...MY CARBURETER IS SHOT, I HEAR YOU'RE A BIG PARTS MERCHANT... GOT ANY?
I NEVER HAVE ANY PROBLEM. IT'S NOT FOR NUTHIN' THAT I'M KNOWN AS TH' BIG FIX OF COMPANY 'B'...I'LL BE RIGHT BACK!

A LITTLE "5 FINGER REQUISITIONING" IS THE SECRET OF MY SUCCESS
?

S'LONG JOE, THANKS.
PRIVATE JOE DOPE!!
?

YOU BEEN CANNIBALIZIN' ON ALL THE VEHICLES IN THE POOL...BUT I NEVER REALIZED WHAT IT COULD LEAD TO UNTIL I TOOK A LOOK AT THE INSIDE OF MY OWN JEEP.... NO ENGINE LEFT!
...FASTER, I GOT TWO MORE STOPS T'MAKE!
PRODUCED UNDER SPECIAL LICENSE TO U. S. DEPT. DEFENSE
COPR. 1951 WILL EISNER PRODUCTIONS

Joe Dope strips No. 9-12, 1951.

JOE DOPE — Salt On His Tail — **By WILL EISNER**

SERGEANT BLUGSCRABBLE, FOR A COMBAT VETERAN WITH A SILVER STAR, YOU SURE ARE NERVOUS.... THIS IS A SIMPLE MISSION OF TAKIN' A TRAILER OF AMMO UP FORWARD ....WHY??

SURE I'M NERVOUS... YOU NEVER HOOKED UP THE SAFETY CHAIN OF THE TRAILER ON THE JEEP!!
AAH... THAT'S A OL' FASHIONED NOTION... I STOPPED DOIN' THAT YEARS AGO!

YES, BUT SUPPOSE THE PINTLE BREAKS?
AHAW... IT'S POSSIBLE.... BUT IT AIN'T EVER HAPPENED TO ME... HEY DID YOU HEAR THAT?
BOOM

THERE'S ALWAYS A FIRST TIME... AND ONCE IS ENOUGH!
13.
PRODUCED UNDER SPECIAL LICENSE TO U. S. DEPT. DEFENSE
COPR. 1951 WILL EISNER PRODUCTIONS

JOE DOPE — That's That — **By WILL EISNER**

WELL SIR, HE STARTED OUT ATOP THIS HILL, AND SEEING HOW STEEP IT WAS, HE SLAMMED ON THE BRAKES!
THAT'S GOOD!

BUT... HE KEPT RIDING THE BRAKE... AS MOST GUYS DO...
THAT'S BAD!
PRODUCED UNDER SPECIAL LICENSE TO U. S. DEPT. DEFENSE
COPR. 1951 WILL EISNER PRODUCTIONS

NOT REALIZING THAT THE BRAKE DRUM WAS GETTING HOT, EXPANDING, AND THUS LOSING IT'S GRIP!
THAT'S RIGHT!

BY THE TIME HE WAS HALF WAY DOWN, HE WAS RIDING WITH NO BRAKE AT ALL!
THAT'S ALL!
14.

JOE DOPE — It's Frammiss No Matter How Y'slice It — **By WILL EISNER**

AHH... LOOKIT THEM GO.... THAT'S FOR ME... YESSIR IT'S IN ME BLOOD... SIX GENERATIONS OF DOPES WUS ALL RACING DRIVERS ...I'M INSPIRED!
JOE... COME ON, WE'RE DUE IN FOR RETREAT IN TWENTY MINUTES!

PRIVATE JOE DOPE, WAAT ARE YOU DOING?
SPEED MY DEAR ONA BALL.... THIS IS A SPEED AGE ....IN A TRICE I'LL TRANSFORM THIS JALOPY TO A HOTROD!
PRODUCED UNDER SPECIAL LICENSE TO U. S. DEPT. DEFENSE
COPR. 1951 WILL EISNER PRODUCTIONS

DO YOU KNOW WHAT YOU'RE DOING?? YOU'RE NOT QUALIFIED TO DO HIGHER ECHELON WORK!
MY DEAR ONA, IT'S A SIMPLE MATTER.... I'M MERLY CAMMING THE FRAMMISS AND GIVING MORE FORTISM TO THE CARBURETOR!
15

HOURS LATER...
ARE YOU SURE YOU USED THE RIGHT FRAMMIS ...BECAUSE IT SEEMS TO ME WE'VE ONLY GOT ONE OR TWO EXHAUST VALVES LEFT!
OK, OK... Y'CAN STOP NEEDLING ME NOW.... WE'RE ALMOST HOME.
CHUG CHUG CHUG

JOE DOPE — Depends On How Y'see Yourself — **By WILL EISNER**

5

PRODUCED UNDER SPECIAL LICENSE TO U. S. DEPT. DEFENSE
COPR. 1951 WILL EISNER PRODUCTIONS

16.

Joe Dope strips No. 13-16, 1951.

JOE DOPE What's Goose For The Gander BY WILL EISNER

YEOW!
SSS
17
Will Eisner

HAW HAW HAW!
LEMME INSIDE QUICK... THAT JOE DOPE IS LOOSE WITH A AIR HOSE AGAIN...
OH, OH, HE'S ONE OF THEM COMEDIANS
PRODUCED UNDER SPECIAL LICENSE TO U. S. DEPT. DEFENSE
COPR. 1951 WILL EISNER PRODUCTIONS

HEE HEE
GASP

YEOW!

HEE HEE... I BEEN THINKIN' JOE. BET A GUY COULD HAVE A LOTTA FUN AROUND THE POOL WITH A AIR HOSE, EH???

JOE DOPE Riding Cheek-To-Cheek By WILL EISNER

...CAAMON! GET MOVIN'...
AREN'T YOU RIDING AWFUL CLOSE, JOE?
18
Will Eisner

SUPPOSE THE MAN AHEAD STOPS SHORT...
THEN I STEP ONNA BRAKE AND STOP TOO! LIKE THIS....

PRODUCED UNDER SPECIAL LICENSE TO U. S. DEPT. DEFENSE
COPR. 1951 WILL EISNER PRODUCTIONS

JOE DOPE Yeah, He Used Clean Dirt... BY WILL EISNER

GREASE
19 Will Eisner

GREASE

GREASE
PRODUCED UNDER SPECIAL LICENSE TO U. S. DEPT. DEFENSE
COPR. 1951 WILL EISNER PRODUCTIONS

ARE YOU SURE YOU CLEANED THAT BEARING?

JOE DOPE We're All Burned Up By WILL EISNER

LIKE I WAS SAYING, JOE...
20

...YOU KEEP RIDING THE CLUTCH....

AAAH..... QUIT PICKIN' ON ME.... IT'S A MATTER OF STYLE... AND THIS IS ME OWN STYLE OF DRIVIN'!

HEY... DO YOU SMELL SOMETHIN' BURNIN'??

YES, ME, THE TAXPAYER... AND YOUR CLUTCH!
PRODUCED UNDER SPECIAL LICENSE TO U. S. DEPT. DEFENSE
COPR. 1951 WILL EISNER PRODUCTIONS

Joe Dope strips No. 17-20, 1951.

HOW A TOUCH-TONE PHONE HELPED PUT THE FINGER ON
RIP ROSCOE
BY Will Eisner
THE DEADLY SPIDER GANG

WHEN I CAME TO... I KNEW I'D BE OKAY BECAUSE I COULD STILL REMEMBER MY NAME RIP ROSCOE I KNEW SOMETHING ELSE TOO...
...IF I DIDN'T FIND A WAY TO BAG MY HOSTS THE DEADLY SPIDER GANG... IT WOULD BE CURTAINS FOR YOURS TRULY
...BUT THEN THERE IT WAS... RIGHT UNDER MY NOSE... A TOUCH-TONE PHONE!!
I KNEW IT CAME IN LOTS OF COLORS WHICH DIDN'T COST EXTRA...
...AND THAT EACH BUTTON MAKES ITS OWN MUSICAL NOTE!
...BUT AT THE MOMENT ALL THAT DIDN'T CONCERN ME!!
...WHAT MATTERED NOW WAS HOW FAST AND EASY A TOUCH-TONE PHONE IS TO DIAL!!

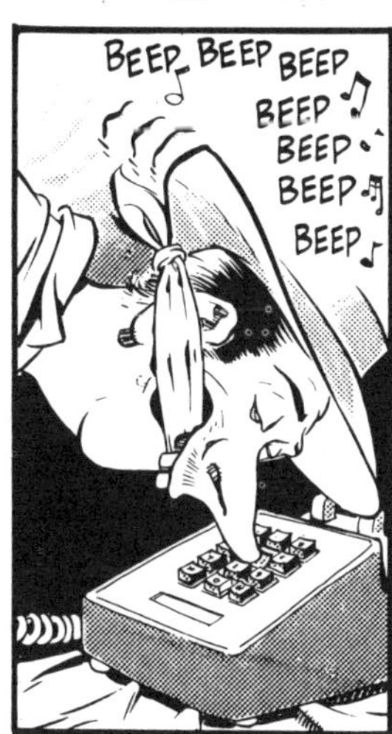
BEEP BEEP BEEP
BEEP
BEEP
BEEP
BEEP

HELLO MARGO... RIP... CALL THE INSPECTOR!! I'M SITTING ON THE SPIDER GANG... BUT I DON'T KNOW HOW MUCH LONGER I CAN HOLD THEM!

TOUCH-TONE SERVICE IS AVAILABLE IN MOST AREAS AT ADDITIONAL COST. A GOOD TIME TO ORDER IS WHEN YOU MOVE. CALL YOUR LOCAL TELEPHONE BUSINESS OFFICE OR ASK YOUR TELEPHONE INSTALLER.

New York Telephone

Rip Roscoe, newspaper advertisement for New York Telephone, 1976.

In addition to his purely commercial work during this period, Eisner also wrote and illustrated a number of humorous cartoon books, among them the four volume *Gleeful Guide* series and several oriented toward the adolescent market which were (and are) sold through school book clubs. The art on these two pages, selected from Will Eisner's *Gleeful Guide to Living with Astrology, How To Avoid Death & Taxes... And Live Forever,* and *Dating and Hanging Out*, represents but a small cross-section of Eisner's playful gag cartoon work.

YOU CAN USUALLY FIND GIRLS WHERE THE BOYS ARE
. . . ACTUALLY, THEY'LL BE ACROSS THE STREET— VERY PREOCCUPIED.
HI, HAVE ANY OF YOU GIRLS SEEN THE GUYS AROUND ?

THE QUESTION IS... DID KIRKEGAARD HAVE THE DEFINITIVE ANSWER?!
...I THINK..?
THE IMPACT OF HIS PHILOSOPHY ON TWENTIETH CENTURY THOUGHT IS CENTRAL TO THE QUESTION!!
TRUE, BUT....
...I THINK YOU'RE WRONG ABOUT KIRKEGAARD...
KIRKEGAARD WHO???

...YOU LOSE BY DEFAULT, JIM!
1995

EAT!
HEY, YOU STUPID, UGLY OAF... WHICH WOULD YOU RATHER DO? ..MAKE LOVE TO ME...OR EAT!!?

The Spirit: 1966-1981

The mid-1960s "camp" craze generated a renaissance of interest in popular culture. Artists like Roy Lichtenstein and Andy Warhol became famous simply for painting enlarged comic book panels and soup can labels. A combination of nostalgia and aesthetic rebellion against the cold formalism of 1950s "modern" art led to the widespread acceptance of, and investment in, "kitsch" and "collectibles." These objects, too new to be antiques, but too vivid, charming or colourful to be consigned to the junkpile, gained the attention of scholars and trend-setters alike. Old comic books, with their bright pages, their evocation of childhood, and their unexpected scarcity, were suddenly valuable collector's items.

Perhaps the first "high brow" recognition of this new fad came in 1965 with the publication of an article by Jules Feiffer in *Playboy* magazine, in which the author recounted his memories of a not-so-halcyon youth in Brooklyn in the years preceeding World War II, naming virtually every comic book he loved. His praise of Eisner's *Spirit* was lavish, and when the article was expanded into a full colour volume entitled *The Great Comic Book Heroes,* Eisner and *The Spirit* were again prominently included. For the first time, a host of young fans had a chance to read a complete *Spirit* story. What they didn't know at the time was that when Feiffer praised the pre-war *Spirit* and curtly passed a negative judgement on its post-war period, it was his own role as the series' scripter he was damning. Ironically, the very *Spirit* story he reprinted was one which he had occasion to rewrite during the post-war era he despised. Of course this deprecatory tongue-in-cheek business was lost on the general reader, who only saw in Feiffer's praise and the story reprinted a precious glimpse into a long-forgotten corner of the comic book world.

Will at his drawing board, 1977.

In any case, the time was right — interest in comics was high — when the New York *Herald Tribune* asked Will to bring *The Spirit* out of retirement in 1966. He gladly complied, producing a five page political satire for the paper's Sunday magazine. That re-appearance was something of a "class re-union," for Feiffer wrote a second article on comics as pop-sociology and Marilyn Mercer, another one-time *Spirit* assistant, wrote an introductory piece on Eisner. As a result of this publicity, the feature picked up even more young readers and was soon being reprinted on a regular basis. The reprints, which began in 1966, continue to this day, spanning a longer time period than the original run of the series covered. They have been accompanied by new cover art, occasional portfolio plates and numerous spot illos featuring *The Spirit*, as well as a couple of all-new stories featuring the masked crime-fighter.

THE SPIRIT
BY Will Eisner
Will Eisner ©76

Cover, *The Spirit, The First 93 Dailies* (Ken Pierce, 1977). Four volumes, collecting the entire run of the daily *Spirit* series, have been published by Ken Pierce as part of his ongoing line of newspaper strip reprints.

SPIRIT
Will Eisner
LIKE A FUNGUS, ON THE STRUCTURE OF EVERY CITY GOVERNMENT, THERE GROWS OVER THE YEARS A SORT OF BUILD-UP OF JOBS. AGENCIES, DEPARTMENTS OR COMMISSIONS WHICH NEVER QUITE END. LONG SINCE HAVING ACCOMPLISHED THE PURPOSE FOR WHICH THEY WERE ORDAINED...THEY CONTINUE ON UNNOTICED AND UNDISTURBED, SNUG IN THE WARM WOMB OF ANONYMITY. AS EACH NEW SUCCESIVE ADMINISTRATION COMES INTO POWER CREATING JOBS OR AGENCIES OF ITS OWN, THE WEB BECOMES MORE COMPLEX! ...AFTER MANY YEARS THESE ZOMBI-LIKE AGENCIES FORM A STRUCTURE OF THEIR OWN--A CELL-LIFE INDEPENDENT OF THE MAIN BODY OF CITY GOVERNMENT...
NOW, INTRICATE, GREEDILY FEEDING AT THE PUBLIC TROUGH, THEY LIE, QUIET AND STILL AS A POISONED WELL, FEARFUL OF ONLY ONE THING...CHANGE!
INTO THIS STAGNANT POOL, ONE NIGHT LAST OCTOBER, A PEBBLE WAS DROPPED AND THE RIPPLES DISTURBED... HOBART NAUGHT ASSISTANT DEPUTY VICE COMMISSIONER FOR THE INVESTIGATION OF INDEFINABLE WASTE (appointed 1933)
HOBART, IT'S ME, MAXWELL MOMZER... OPEN UP... I GOT TERRIBLE NEWS!!
KNOK KNOK
THE... REPORT... IT SAYS LINDSAY WILL WIN!!! THE MAYORLTY!
NO! NO!
GLAK
SHADDAP... I'VE GOT TO THINK!
HOBART YOU KNOW WHAT THIS MEANS... THEY'LL START SHAKING UP DEPARTMENTS... SOMEBODY WILL ASK WHAT WE DO HERE!
I KNOW... I KNOW... THIRTY-TWO YEARS OF JOB SECURITY WILL GO DOWN THE DRAIN... NO SIR, I'LL NOT TAKE THIS LYING DOWN!
WE WILL STOP LINDSAY ONE-WAY-OR-THE-OTHER. COME ON!!
DON'T WORRY, MAXWELL... DON'T WORRY
CRAK

Splash page, *The Spirit*, January 9, 1966. This story only appeared in the New York *Herald Tribune*.

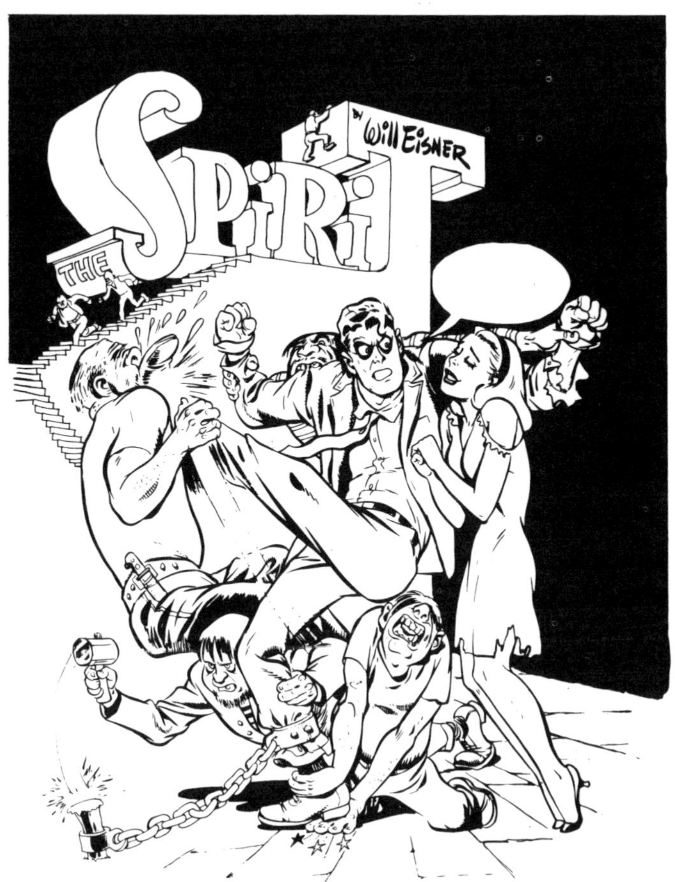
THE SPIRIT
by Will Eisner

Cover, *The Spirit* No. 1 (Harvey, October, 1966).

A little over thirteen years after the last *Spirit Section* had been published, Eisner revived the character for an apocryphal five page story which ran in the New York *Herald Tribune's* Sunday *New York* magazine. The plot, which revolves around Mayor John Lindsay's bid for re-election amidst the murderous intrigues of feather-bedding petty bureaucrats, is set in New York rather than Eisner's mythical Central City. Furthermore, Ellen Dolan, who in 1950 had been elected Mayor of Central City, appears here as a small-time government secretary, while Ebony White, now a corpulent adult, is a social worker in Harlem. The script was written by Eisner and he pencilled it, but the inking is by Chuck Kramer. Kramer worked on *P*S* magazine and had a style very similar to Will's when it came to humorous subjects, but on the more serious passages of this story, the disparity between their approaches is readily evident.

Following the success of the *Herald Tribune* story, Harvey Comics published two issues of *The Spirit* in 1966 and 1967. Each of these contained an all-new seven-page lead story written and pencilled by Eisner and inked by Chuck Kramer. The feature then lay dormant until 1972, when Kitchen Sink revived it in "underground" format. Publication of the collected daily *Spirit* strip and continuous reprints of the Sunday *Spirit Sections* have continued unabated since then, not only in America but in France, Mexico, Germany, Italy, Holland, Denmark, Sweden, Spain, Brazil, and England. Many of these reprints required new cover art. Rough pencils and finished art for a few of these covers appear on this and the next seven pages.

50¢
SNARF
ADULTS ONLY!
NO. 3
KITCHEN SINK ENTERPRISES
I'M GONNA ARREST 'EM SPIRIT!
...FOR WHAT DOLAN?
YOU'RE BEGINNING TO SHOW ESTABLISHMENT TENDENCIES ..WATCH IT HOBART!
KRUPP COM WCD
HOW DO YOU SPELL... ER, DEFECATE?
SCREW IT ALL
...AFTER CRUMB WHAT IS THERE LEFT TO SAY?
I HAVE JUST DISCOVERED A HORRIBLE THING - WE ARE THE ESTABLISHMENT!
Will Eisner © 1972

Cover, *Snarf* No. 3 (Kitchen Sink, November, 1972). *Snarf* features the work of popular underground cartoonists, but on occasion editor-publisher Denis Kitchen has commissioned work by the likes of Eisner and Harvey Kurtzman, who don't usually appear in this field.

Cover, *The Spirit* No. 1 (Kitchen Sink, January, 1973).

Cover, *The Spirit* No. 2 (Kitchen Sink, September, 1973).

WARREN MAGAZINE
SPIRIT
#3
AUG. 1974
THE SPIRIT
Will Eisner
59296-5
PDC
$1.00
DEATH RIDES THE RAILS... WHEN THE SPIRIT FIGHTS FOR HIS LIFE AGAINST A HIRED KILLER!
8 CLASSIC STORIES OF HORROR AND SUSPENSE!
Will Eisner
RETAILERS: SEE PAGE 69 FOR DISPLAY ALLOWANCE PLAN

Cover, *The Spirit* No. 3 (Warren, August, 1974). The finished piece was coloured by Richard Corben.

Cover rough, *The Spirit* No. 7 (Warren, April, 1975).

Cover rough, *Tintin* (France, mid-1970s).

Cover rough, *Tintin* (France, mid-1970s).

Cover rough, *The Spirit* No. 5 (Warren, December 1974).

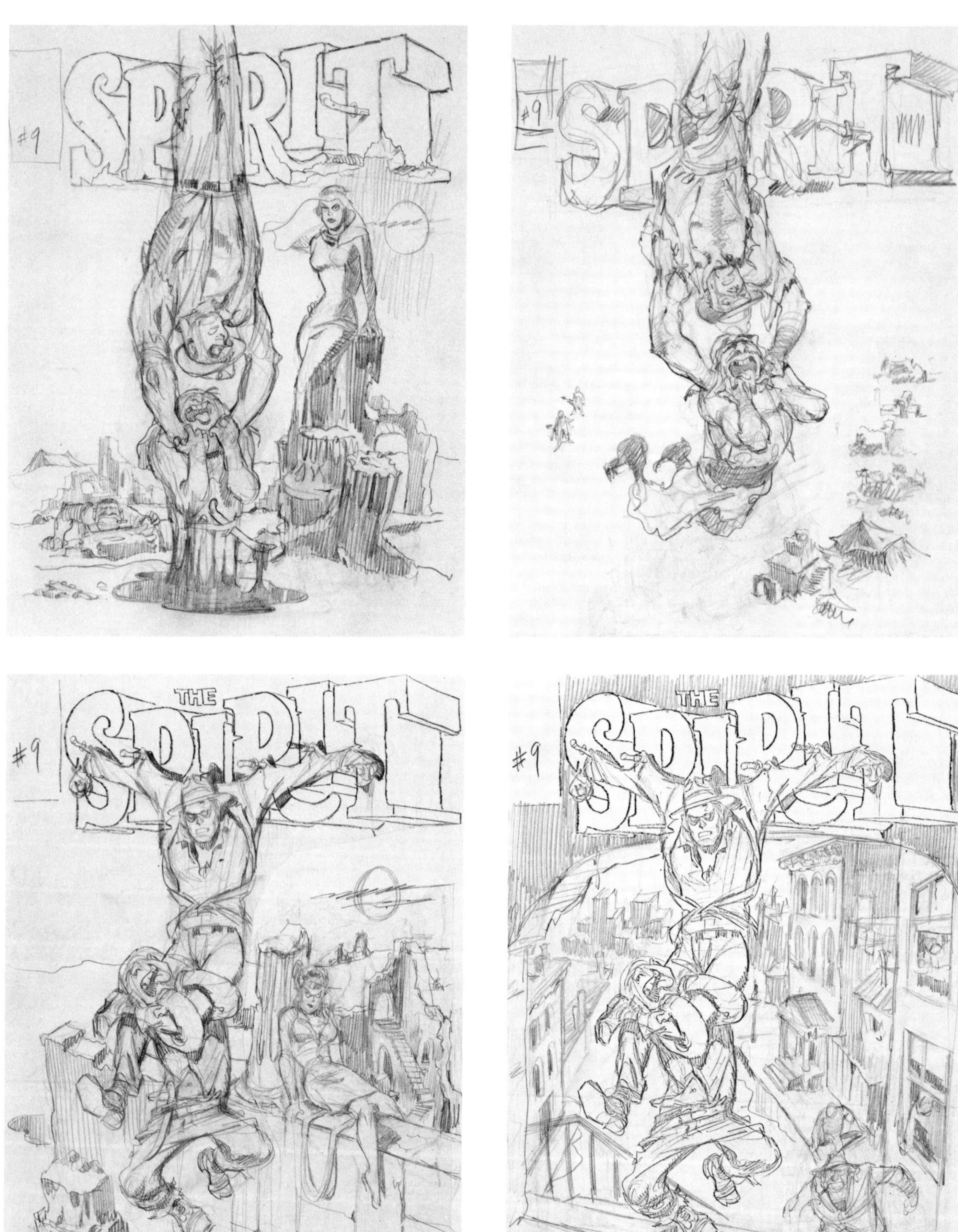

Four successive cover roughs, *The Spirit* No. 9 (Warren, August, 1975). The original concept, featuring P'Gell and an Arab, was based on an interior story. The final, published version at right utilizes only the major figures and has been translocated into Eisner's familiar tenement district.

Cover, *The Spirit* No. 9 (Warren, August, 1975). The finished piece was coloured by Ken Kelly.

Four successive cover roughs, *The Spirit* No. 11 (Warren, December, 1975). These cover ideas are based on the March 12, 1950 story, *The Jewel*. The finished cover bears no resemblance at all to the sketches.

I CAME TO YOUR HOUSE AS A FRIEND AND YOU MURDERED ME!!...FOR THIS MAY YOUR PEOPLE BE PARALYZED BY THE STAIN OF MY BLOOD

IF YOU HAVE ANY DOUBTS TAKE THE HIGH ROAD FROM BALA IN MERIONETHSHIRE, WALES ONE NIGHT AND SEE FOR YOURSELF ... HAVE NO FEAR IT'S A GOOD GHOST THAT PATROLS THE ROAD

Two pages from Will Eisner's *Spirit Casebook of True Haunted Houses and Ghosts*, 1976. This volume is not a *Spirit* story in any sense of the word. It is instead a series of famous and purportedly true accounts of hauntings, poltergeists and the like, each one illustrated by Eisner and supplied with a narrative introduction by The Spirit. Although most of the book is typeset rather than hand lettered, The Spirit's monologues appear in conventional comic book word balloons.

THE SPIRIT
BY
Will Eisner

SMOKE-FILLED ROOM

PLATFORM COMMITTEE

VOTE GOP

Editorial cartoon for the New York *Times*, August 16, 1976. Although this strip is titled *The Spirit*, it is not the ghost of Denny Colt who haunts the smoke-filled room and platform committee of the Republican Party's national convention.

In recent years Will has drawn numerous small pieces best described as "incidental" *Spirit* art. Most of them are simple ink sketches, produced for friends, fans, convention program books and fanzines. A few of the hundreds of such known drawings are shown on this and the facing page.

SPIRIT
Will Eisner
COMICS
COMICS
©1974 W.E

Drawing done for a comic book convention program booklet, 1974.

SORRY I CAN'T ATTEND THE SAN DIEGO CON' THIS YEAR SHEL... I'M ALL TIED UP!
Will Eisner

Drawing done for a comic book convention program booklet, 1981.

WHERE DID YOU SAY WE WERE, SPIRIT??
...KANSAS CITY... I THINK, BATMAN!
JERRY ROBINSON & Will Eisner

In 1979, Eisner and former Batman artist Jerry Robinson spoke at Johnson County Community College in Overland Park, Kansas, a suburb of Kansas City. This "jam" page, in which Robinson drew The Batman and Eisner did The Spirit, arose from that experience.

CRIME IN THE COMICS
Will Eisner
©1978

Illustration for an article by Maurice Horn in *The American Cartoonist*, a publication of the National Cartoonists Society, 1978.

Cover, *The Buyer's Guide for Comic Fandom*, 1974. *The Buyer's Guide* is a weekly tabloid which carries news of upcoming comics and advertisements for old comics, gum cards, radio show premiums and other nostalgic collectibles. Although this cover was drawn in 1974, Eisner misplaced it and it was not found until this book was in production! It was finally printed in *The Buyer's Guide* in 1981.

Drawing done for a fan, 1975.

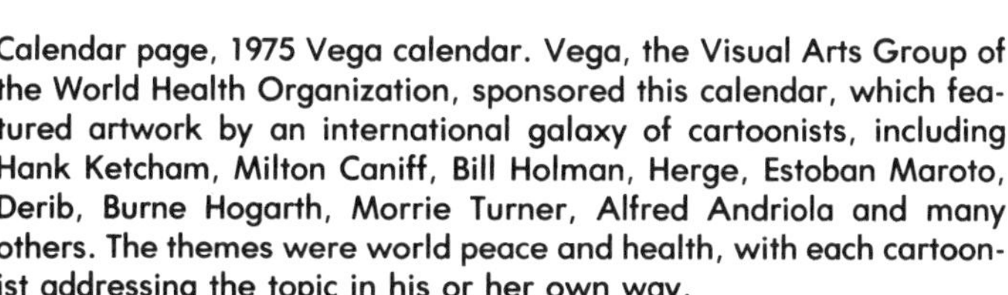

Calendar page, 1975 Vega calendar. Vega, the Visual Arts Group of the World Health Organization, sponsored this calendar, which featured artwork by an international galaxy of cartoonists, including Hank Ketcham, Milton Caniff, Bill Holman, Herge, Estoban Maroto, Derib, Burne Hogarth, Morrie Turner, Alfred Andriola and many others. The themes were world peace and health, with each cartoonist addressing the topic in his or her own way.

The Convention, plate No. 6 from *The Spirit Portfolio* (Collector's Press, 1977). This painting, with its cryptic allusions to the traditional symbolism found in medieval and Renaissance crucifixion scenes, is one of Will's most enigmatic works.

Wraparound cover for *The Spirit* No. 26 (Kitchen Sink, December 1980).

Wraparound cover for *The Spirit* No. 30 (Kitchen Sink, August 1981). The issue featured a new Spirit story done in "jam" style by fifty artists and writers. The cover was also a jam. Eisner inked the Spirit and the women flanking him — Nylon Rose and Silk Satin. The rest of this cover was inked by Milton Caniff, John Pound, Richard Corben, Leslie Cabarga, Denis Kitchen and Peter Poplaski. Poplaski also pencilled this cover.

GERMANY
TURN OFF THE HEADLIGHTS ...I'LL USE MY FLASH !!
BLUDD!!?
TOMKINS?
I'VE GOT MALLEY AND ARGANO... I BROUGHT THEM OUT AS I PROMISED, BLUDD!!
OVER HERE, TOMKINS,... WHERE WE CAN TALK!

A page from Chapter 3, *Life On Another Planet*, published in *The Spirit* No. 21 (Kitchen Sink, July, 1979). This 128 page adventure story stars Jim Bludd, an astrophysicist-turned-spy who ultimately decides to sabotage the project he has been hired to protect.

LIFE ON ANOTHER PLANET 6
I CAN'T SIT IN THIS SHACK FOREVER WHILE THEY BUILD-UP THAT LAUNCH!
I'M HERE TO STOP THIS INSANE LAUNCH UNTIL THE NATIONS CAN UNIFY BEHIND THIS PROJECT
AND I NEED YOU TO HELP ME STOP THE LAUNCH IN ANY WAY WE CAN
ANY WAY? ??? SO, BLOW UP THE FRIGGIN' JOINT!
NO, NO, NO! I JUST CAN'T KILL MANY HUNDREDS OF INNOCENT WORKERS!
...THERE MUST BE ANOTHER WAY...
SHEEUT.... I GOT ME A FRIGGIN' NOBLEMAN ...HOO!!
SHEEEEUT!

Splash page, Chapter 6, *Life On Another Planet*, published in *The Spirit* No. 24 (Kitchen Sink, May, 1980). There were a total of 8 sixteen-page chapters in this story, and they appeared in *The Spirit* magazine No. 19 through 26.

Plate for the National Cartoonists Society portfolio, 1980.

The Remembered Ghetto: 1978-1981

Will Eisner has always been an innovator. Repetition of ideas has never suited his personality. Having pioneered in package shop production of original comic book art during the 1930s, he abandoned the field completely for the development of the *Spirit* newspaper supplement in 1940. Once drafted into the War, he turned his attention to the brand new area of educational comics and convinced a highly skeptical Pentagon to employ his talents as a "salesman" for preventive maintenance. With the War over, Eisner did not so much return to *The Spirit* as renovate it, giving it a new graphic style and an entirely different literary tone. Simultaneously, he branched out into the field of "reading rack" comics, giveaways and semi-technical material. Once he had that genre firmly in his grasp, he began to draw gag cartoons and joke books. The desire to pioneer new forms is as central to Eisner's aesthetic as his obvious concerns with social justice, emotional depth of characterization and startling visual trickery.

Thus, when *The Spirit* was revived in the late 1960s, Will went along with the trend, but not wholeheartedly. New *Spirit* covers appeared with regularity, but when fans asked him, over and over again to give them a steady stream of fresh *Spirit* stories, he always answered them with a question: "Why?"

It was a rhetorical question at best. Eisner, his strong personal identification with his fictional character intact after all the years, was really concerned with a deeper problem. "I was always Denny Colt," he would say, "but now I seem to look like Commissioner Dolan," and he would laugh in his very genial and engaging way. Or, putting on a veneer of disarming intensity, he would lean forward and look the fan dead in the eyes. "Why do you want new *Spirit* stories? Have you read all of the old ones? Do you like the character that much? Or is it the mood, the atmosphere of the forties, the crime fighting?" He had no patience for the confused answers the fans would return. No consensus satisfied him because none addressed the hidden question: can — or should — a man in his sixties occupy his time meaningfully by spinning out heroic fantasies about a costumed do-gooder half his age? Isn't there something more, something better, to be done with the sequential art form, something beyond romantic escape fiction?

By 1978, he seemed to have finally answered his own question. The answer was "Yes."

One of the elements which gave *The Spirit* its long-term appeal was Eisner's loving and passionate homages to the city he was born and raised in. New York, or more properly, Brooklyn and The Bronx, was, in Eisner's metaphoric world, transformed into a stage upon which the most wide-sweeping and the most intimate dramas of human life were enacted. His elaborate architectural renderings, his startling use of false perspective, and his tender glimpses into the lives of the city's poor were integral to the ambience in which The Spirit dwelled. In the end, after the symbolic activity of crime-fighting was dispelled, the city and its fragile human contents were all that remained.

Will Eisner, 1980.

As if in obedience to a well-crafted "Eisnerian" plot-line, Will's approach to his art has come full circle. Having removed the fantasy element from his work, he is currently occupied with the creation of portfolios and narratives which present a pure, clear and persistent vision of the tenements and the people he first began to draw when he was fifteen years old.

The "forgotten ghetto" wasn't forgotten after all, it seems.

Family, a plate from *City, A Narrative Portfolio* (Hollybrook Graphics, 1980). This portfolio, limited to 1500 signed copies, contains six plates, each accompanied by an illustrated poem.

Page 9, *The Treasure of Avenue 'C'*, one of the stories in Eisner's current work-in-progress, *The Big City: A Portrait.* This chapter was published in *The Spirit* No. 27 (Kitchen Sink, February, 1981). The completed book will contain over a dozen chapters, each one dealing with the interaction between the people who live in the 'Big City' and the architectural landmarks which surround them. In this instance, the actions of the narrative are centered around a subway grate.

IF GOD REQUIRES THAT MEN HONOR THEIR AGREEMENTS...
...THEN IS NOT GOD, ALSO, SO OBLIGATED ??

I ASK YOU...WERE THE TERMS NOT CLEARLY WRITTEN ??
...DID I IGNORE EVEN ONE TINY SENTENCE - OR PERHAPS A SINGLE COMMA ?

ENOUGH

Three pages from the title story, *A Contract With God* (Baronet, 1978).

In 1978, Baronet Books published Eisner's *A Contract With God And Other Tenement Stories,* a 192 page "graphic narrative." Will had worked on it for two years in relative silence and its appearance was completely unexpected by his fans, who were convinced he had abandoned sequential comics in favour of gag cartoons.

The four short stories which comprise *A Contract With God* are universal in scope but personal in the sense that they arise from Eisner's own experiences. Set in the 1930s in a tenement, they are what Will calls "eyewitness fiction." The fictional veil is thinnest of all in the last story of the quartet, *Cookelein,* which relates in detail the events which transpire during the fifteenth summer of an introspective boy named Willie.

When asked if the piece is indeed autobiographical, Will laughs. "Sure...it's me," he says. "Or someone like me...or someone I might have known...someone called Willie, anyway."

No one knew much about them...

Page from *The Street Singer, A Contract With God* (Baronet, 1978).

The super at 55 Dropsie was Mr. Scuggs.
MISTER SCUGGS, WHEN YOU GONNA FIX THE HALL STEPS? WHAT KINDA BUILDING YOU RUNNIN' HA??
Nobody really liked Mr. Scuggs.

I'M RUNNING THIS BUILDING MR. LEVINSKY! AND I'LL DECIDE WHEN THINGS NEED TO BE FIXED!
Infact they were a little afraid of him...why, who knows?

Perhaps it was what they **didn't** know that fed the fear.
TENANTS... PTOOY!!

YAH!... BACK IN CHERMANY THINGS IS DIFFERENT! THERE, THEY HAF **RESPECT**! YAH, **THERE** NOBODY TALKS LIKE THAT TO THE SUPER!
SOON, SOMEDAY WE WILL HAVE DISCIPLINE HERE TOO! YAH, ITS COMING ...ORDNUNG!

Four Pages from *The Super, A Contract With God* (Baronet, 1978). In this volume Eisner made extensive use of full-page story panels, a decision prompted in part by the smaller page size of the paperback format.

NOO,..WILLIE? VACATIONS OVER ALREADY! SO, START GETTING READY FOR SCHOOL!! THIS YEAR YOU'RE GONNA HAVE LOTSA RESPONSIBILITY AROUND HERE...YOUR FATHER IS.... ...GONNA BE AH TRAVELLING A LOT,..SO,YIZZEL BE THE MAN OF THE HOUSE NOW!..Y'HEAR ME WILLIE...WILLIE?

Final page, *Cookelein, A Contract With God* (Baronet, 1978).

The following collections of Will Eisner's work may be of interest to those who enjoyed this volume:

Will Eisner's Spirit Magazine, published bi-monthly by Kitchen Sink, No. 2 Swamp Road, Princeton, Wis. 54968. This periodical reprints classic Sunday stories, one of which is in full color each issue. It also publishes new work by Eisner, essays on comic art, interviews with well-known cartoonists and other Eisner-related material. Subscription is $18/year (6 issues) in North America. Foreign subscriptions are $21/year via seamail or $28 airmail.

The Spirit Dailies (four volumes), published by Ken Pierce, P.O. Box 332, Park Forest, Ill. 60466. Send a first class postage stamp for details on these and other newspaper strip reprints available.

Spirit Color Album, Volume I, published by Kitchen Sink Press, No. 2 Swamp Road, Princeton, Wis. 54968. This hard-cover book reprints thirteen *Spirit* stories in full colour. $12.50 postpaid.

Will Eisner Color Treasury, published by Kitchen Sink Press, No. 2 Swamp Road, Princeton, Wis. 54968. A 112-page hardcover collection of two *Spirit* stories, twenty-five *Spirit* magazine covers (many recoloured by Eisner), all sixteen of Eisner's portfolio plates and other Eisner art, nearly all of which is reproduced in color. $14.50 postpaid.